The
Friendship
Book

**A THOUGHT
FOR EACH DAY** | **2024**

January

FRIDA and her family decided to start the year with a breath of fresh air after spending so long indoors.

Making the most of the few hours of sunshine available in the north-east of Scotland at that time of year, they drove to a nearby headland and found a picnic bench overlooking the North Sea.

Deciding to forgo fine dining, and maybe even table manners, Frida opened a tub of sandwiches.

She turned to look for the flasks, and a gust of wind blew the plastic tub off the table, sending the sandwiches dancing across the grass. Two or three disappeared over the cliff edge.

Deciding that perhaps it was best to head home, but still wanting to make something of the day, she suggested the family pick up the remnants of their lunch, name them after something bad that happened the previous year, and bin them!

Then they stood hand in hand near the cliff edge and let the wind blow away the hurts and regrets of the last 12 months.

They were hungry and dishevelled when they got home, but those things were quickly dealt with.

What didn't change so quickly was the lightness of spirit they all felt.

Tuesday – January 2

I MET Robert on the path between the carpark and his house.

"I just put the handbrake on, turned the engine off, and then I sat a moment, thinking of the kind and helpful people I'd met in the shops and on the road," he said.

"Then I looked at the clock and saw it was just short of twelve noon. I thought, 'Well played, Tuesday!'"

With that kind of appreciation, I'm quite sure Robert's day only got better!

Wednesday – January 3

TIME is such a precious gift –
Don't let it slip away.
Make the most of every moment;
Always seize the day.

When the world looks gloomy
And the sun forgets to shine,
Keep busy and keep cheerful
Until things turn out fine.

When happiness uplifts your heart
And helps your spirit climb,
Then keep it safe and seize the day
And cherish precious time.

Iris Hesselden

Thursday – January 4

I WAS running late for a funeral and kicking myself. I had no good excuse.

Arriving just ahead of the undertakers, I saw a man hesitate, then turn away from the church gates.

At the risk of being even later, I asked if he was OK.

"I really wanted to go in to pay my respects," he told me. "But look at me! I have no smart clothes and I didn't want to be disrespectful."

I took his arm and led him back towards the door.

"Actually," I told him, "the family requested casual dress. And here I am in a suit! If you come in with me it might make me look less out of place!"

Was that the reason I was late? Was there a purpose I wasn't aware of? Is God in our lives to such a degree?

I don't know, but I do know that the more I look for him, the more I find him.

I was late to that realisation in my life as well, but I'm glad I got there.

Lighten your spirit and blow away the cobwebs of the old year.

Friday – January 5

SEVERAL people had annoyed me that morning. Afterwards, I caught up with our dear friend, Mary, and asked her if she didn't get days like that as well.

"You know, days when everyone just seems set on frustrating you," I explained. "Surely it's not only me."

To my surprise, she changed the subject by asking how things were with me. She's not normally so rude, so I talked about a couple of things that were concerning me.

Yesterday the bus driver was quite curt with me, the man in the shop seemed like he could take my custom or leave it, and a boy on a bike cut in front of me, scaring the wits out of me.

As I told Mary about it all, she listened patiently.

"And how are things with you, Francis?" she asked.

I made the connection on the way home. What a coincidence, I thought, that on the days when everyone else seemed so contrary, I had worries on my mind!

Perhaps I'll ask her about that when I see her again. Or perhaps I'll just stop projecting my grumpiness on to others.

Saturday – January 6

THE name Ashley Courtenay has been associated with hotel guides since the 1940s.

The 1944 edition of "Let's Halt Awhile" bears the subtitle "Personal Recommendations On Where To Spend Your Leave", because, of course, the world was at war.

At the end of that compilation of beautiful places to stay and relaxing places to visit was, at the author's insistence, an advertisement in which the Red Cross sought donations for the relief of British prisoners of war.

"The next time you're feeling browned off yourself," it read, "remember that your daily routine would seem like paradise to those fellows."

It's a thought that holds true today. How much do we take for granted? How many of the things we complain about would be warmly received by those who have less?

Let's halt awhile and spend some time in appreciation.

Sunday – January 7

MY morning walk around the park was more like a walk through ground-level cloud.

The wind, instead of clearing the air, simply blew the precipitation – can we call it rain if it hasn't left the cloud? – into my face.

Cap pulled down and shoulders hunched, I battled on.

Then I saw a warm yellow light where none ought to be.

Closer now, I realised that it was the star on top of the local council's Christmas tree.

It was still lit, despite the 12 days of Christmas being over.

Past its time, but still a light in the dark. I wondered if this was an apt metaphor, or if I was taking it too far.

It depended, I thought, on whether or not I believed there always was a light in the darkness.

And, there and then, in the cold, the wet and the dark, I knew that I did.

"And the light shineth in darkness; and the darkness comprehended it not."

Monday – January 8

MANY of us were taught Pythagoras's theorem at school. Some even learned it!

But the great mathematician also designed a very special cup.

Filled up to a certain point, it works like any other cup.

But if it is filled beyond that point, a syphon effect empties the whole cup through its base.

This means that the person who tries to take too much to drink is left with nothing at all.

He called it the Cup of Greed, and the concept reminds me of an expression of my mother's when she would say she'd eaten "a plentiful sufficiency".

I rather think she meant she had eaten what was left after the family was fed, bless her.

But the notion that "sufficient" is "plenty", or enough is enough, is surely one that Pythagoras would have agreed with.

11

Tuesday – January 9

I **ASKED** Nigel how he was doing.

"A little embarrassed actually," he told me. "The year has got off to a rocky start for some folk, but I'm just rolling along nicely."

"Sure," I replied. "But you've had difficult times, too."

He thought for a moment, then said, "No. Not really."

The point is, Nigel has had his trials.

He habitually looks for the positive and doesn't dwell on the negative, so he doesn't remember those difficult times.

Looking on the positive side is no more or less real and honest than looking on the negative side. It is a choice.

Guess which option leads to the happier life?

Wednesday – January 10

T **WO-YEAR-OLD** Alex has a fascination for the moon.
Most evenings he will ask his mum or dad where it is, and they will take him into the back garden to look for it.

He has loved seeing it wax and wane, and take rests. On nights when it ought to be there but can't be seen, they explain that it is behind the clouds, and that the clouds will soon blow away.

A lesson that will, I firmly believe, shine bright through any difficulties young Alex might encounter in life.

The light is still there, whether we can see it or not!

Thursday – January 11

D **AVIE** was telling me about the imminent arrival of his 10th grandchild.

"Wow!" I replied. "You have your hands full. How do you cope?"

"Happily," he assured me. "Each and every one of them knows that they are my favourite!"

"Ah." I smiled. "That's the trick, is it?"

His expression turned puzzled, then serious.

"It's no trick," he said. "Each and every one of them is!"

Grandparents, I am sure, will understand.

A grandparent knows how to make all of their young relatives feel special.

Friday – January 12

JEANNIE has had a passion for horse-riding since she was a child. She told me she'd had a leather-worker make a specialist attachment for her saddle recently.

She was delighted with the neatness and detail in the end result and told him she thought it was perfect.

"Well," he replied, straight-faced. "No-one ever showed me how to do it any other way than perfect."

Jeannie's not convinced he wasn't teasing, but the point he made was well received. The examples we set are important.

Saturday – January 13

I DON'T know who first came up with the notion, but it has become such a well-known saying that it is almost accepted as a truth.

I'm talking about the notion that absolute power corrupts, absolutely.

If it is true, and I don't doubt it is, then surely it should make us wonder what would absolute love do, and encourage us to do our best to find out!

Sunday – January 14

JAMES MONTGOMERY was a Scottish-born, Sheffield-based hymn-writer.

He is most known for the hymn "Angels From The Realms Of Glory", but as a journalist and poet he often took on humanitarian causes. He campaigned to prevent children being employed as chimney sweeps.

His writing frequently offended powerful people and, in 1797, he was jailed for a poem criticising the use of force to break up a political gathering.

He used his time of incarceration to compile a book of poems called "Prison Amusements". It made him quite a bit of money!

He is remembered for the beauty of his hymns, but perhaps James Montgomery should also be remembered as a fine example of how to turn a problem into a blessing!

Monday – January 15

THE joiner's van pulled up outside the house. The joiner braced himself against the side of it and boosted his apprentice up on to the roof.

Once up, the apprentice loosened the ties that held a wooden staircase in place and slid the staircase over the end of the van.

The joiner caught the end closest to him, lowered it to the ground, then braced a foot against it.

Then the apprentice walked down the stairs.

"Let that be a lesson to you, lad," the joiner said, laughing. "You make your own path, so it's best you make it well!"

Tuesday – January 16

WE were in a theatre foyer, where a boy was browsing on his tablet, and I heard his mother speak.

"If it looks too good to be true, it probably is," his mother said.

Sensible words.

The Lady Of The House and I had bought chocolates for a young friend who couldn't make the show, so I asked the mother if her son might like them.

I didn't want to undermine her advice, especially with regards to the internet, but I wanted him to know that, sometimes, good things just happen – and that is true.

Wednesday – January 17

THE dry-stone dyke was four feet tall and it had a doorway in it. A gap had been left at the bottom.

Halfway up the wall a long, flat stone had been laid across the gap and more stones were placed on top of it.

I've seen them a few times in older walls. The long stone is called a "lunkie", and the point of the doorway is to allow smaller farm animals to pass through, while keeping larger cattle in.

Whenever we build walls in our lives, we should take a tip from those "dykers", and remember what we want to come in as well as what we want to keep out.

Thursday – January 18

IT has been a wild morning out there. But not everywhere. On the windward side of the house, I can hear the "storm".

In contrast, on the leeward side of the house I can hear a bird singing.

It reminds me that if we make a stand on something, it will usually instigate a lot of huffing and puffing from others, often for no good reason and to no good purpose.

But if it's a stance worth taking, someone will be sheltered by it, and may even sing because of it.

Friday – January 19

ON this bleak wintry day, the bush seemed composed entirely of thorns.

I gave it a wide berth. But, as I walked, I dredged a piece of trivia from the depths of my mind.

Thorn bushes and rose bushes generally belong to the same family.

One majors in beauty and flowers; the other majors in defence and thorns. Basically the same, but reacting differently to life.

Not so different from people. Except that people can choose!

Saturday – January 20

VICKY has a stick. It is about 10 inches long, sharpened at one end and blunter at the other.

Both ends are stained with black ink.

"It used to be a paintbrush," she explained to me. "And then it broke.

"I started using it for drawing in ink, pulling out fine lines with one end and thicker streaks with the other.

"The funny thing is, I have no memory of using it as a paintbrush, but it has been invaluable for years the way it is now."

Sometimes, what we think breaks us only reveals our new – and, perhaps, true – purpose.

Sunday – January 21

SILVER raindrops falling
Like diamonds from the sky;
Crystal snowflakes drifting,
White icing floating by.
Balls of hail are landing
Like heavy little stones;
Crusts of frost are forming,
Such tiny, brittle bones.
Breaths of grey wind gusting
And through the air a chill,
Freezing fog comes tumbling,
While nature stands stock still.

Lily Christie

Monday – January 22

AMANDA was doing the homework from her writing group. The tutor had asked them to describe their favourite "special places".

She found the exercise quite easy, and wrote up a dozen examples. Rereading them, she noticed the names of certain friends and family kept popping up.

"I could only really conclude from this," she told me, "that I don't actually have special places in my life.

"I have special people, and whenever I am with them, the place we are becomes a special place."

Tuesday – January 23

HE was describing his journey from Honduras to the UK.

"My family all live in the same valley. In the valley you are sheltered, comfortable, everything is familiar.

"To get out the valley is a tough climb, you feel lonely, the wind blows you about. But maybe it helps you fly, too.

"And outside of the valley is the whole world!"

His English was a work in progress, so I'm not sure if his story was about a literal or metaphorical valley. Either way, I liked it.

Wednesday – January 24

HE was there for his fence-building skills, not his diplomatic skills. The fence around my friend's garden was made for privacy. The slats overlapped, with no gaps, which meant it caught a lot of wind.

When it came down in a storm, she saw the framework behind the slats wasn't up to the job: the wrong wood, the wrong sizes, and pieces cobbled together, meaning they weren't much use.

"I had no idea," she told him.

"I bet your neighbours did," he replied. "They'd have looked at this mess every day."

Often, seeing things from other people's point of view can benefit everyone.

Thursday – January 25

I WASN'T paying attention as the little lad walked shyly past. "Hey!" I cried, suddenly spotting his kilt. "Looking good!"

His mum, walking a distance behind, explained.

"He wanted to wear it to school for Burns Day, but he wanted to come in early in so he wouldn't meet too many people who might laugh at him. But everyone's been really kind!"

Here's to a world where all the tim'rous beasties can wear what they like!

Friday – January 26

I OFTEN see that little-girl twinkle in her eye, so I listened closely when someone asked our dear friend Mary what her favourite age had been.

In other words, what age was she in her heart.

"This age," she replied. "I am loving being the age I am right now, but I define it my own way.

"Whoever thought they could say you have to be a certain way at a certain age? Who has that kind of authority?

"I am the age I am, and I define it the way that feels best to me."

We all, in our different ages, thought about this, then nodded.

OUR lives are full and busy, and sometimes we need to stop
To remember all the good in life and give thanks for our lot.
There are so many people who give their all each day.
We should never let them slip our minds and thank them when
we pray.
Nurses, doctors, armed forces, and emergency services, too.
Too numerous to mention, those who care for me and you.
Their calling to their country is given without doubt;
They run towards the danger when others just want out.

And in those conversations, lest we should forget,
We must also say a thank you to the people we have met.
Who support us through the hardest times, in places strange
and fearful,
Who hold our hands and comfort us when we are lost and tearful.
Our thankful prayers we offer to friends and family so dear,
And for the love, empowering us to hold them ever near.
A word of thanks for your own life, so precious on this Earth.
Into a world so glorious from the moment of our birth.

Elizabeth McGinty

Sunday – January 28

GIOVANNI GUARESCHI was an Italian humourist and satirist who knew hard times in his early adulthood.

In his book "The House That Nino Built", Nino's family are moving house and his wife is deciding what should go with them and what should be left behind. Suddenly, everything seems essential.

"I thought that if I didn't have all my books and a certain kind of 'atmosphere' around me, I couldn't write," Nino says.

"Then, all of a sudden, I found myself deported and in a concentration camp with nothing but the clothes on my back.

"Then and there I found out what things were really essential to existence and, with God's help, I managed to put them together and live, and think, and write, just as I had before."

Nino's essentials filled a very small bag. Most of ours would, too.

If we ask, God will surely help us find them amongst all the clutter.

Monday – January 29

WHEN she was six, there was something Emma didn't want to do. She wrote it in large letters across a page of her mother's notebook.

Emma is ten now, but her mother, Jamie, still has that page.

"She told me what she wanted – or didn't want," Jamie said. "But she also coloured the words in beautifully and decorated all around them.

"It's a reminder for me that we can disagree, we can express our feelings, we can make our voice heard, but those don't need to be ugly things. We can still do all of that, but with style!"

Tuesday – January 30

I COULD easily have imagined him in Army uniform – tall, fit, muscular. He stepped out his car and the golden retriever pup I was walking made straight for him.

I pulled on her lead to stop her, but he said, "No. Let her. Please."

I did. They spent a couple of minutes making a fuss of each other.

Then he put his hard hat on, climbed into his digger and, as far as I could tell, spent the rest of the day digging ditches through tarmac, concrete and rubble.

I couldn't help but wonder what a moment of mutual affection and appreciation added to that sort of day.

Hard and soft, we need both to make a well-rounded day.

Toughness and tenderness, we need both to make a well-rounded human being.

Wednesday – January 31

AT this time of year, our garden probably looks at its worst: bare, washed out, colourless. Nothing is anywhere near budding.

We had an unexpected fall of snow and it lay for a day. For that day the garden was a delight to look at!

It reminded me of these words, often credited to poet Kahlil Gibran, but they could be a universal truth for all I know.

"Kindness is like snow; it beautifies everything it covers."

A moment of affection with a furry friend can brighten any day.

February

Thursday – February 1

THE little cottage had a sign by the door, naming it Glebeland House.

I've seen enough Glebe Streets, Glebe Avenues, etc, to have looked it up long ago. A "glebe" was a piece of land, often with a house, given by a landowner for the local minister to live on.

I don't know where the word itself comes from. It occurred to me as I looked at the cottage that it might be a contraction of the German "Gott Liebe", or "God love".

Not many of us will get to live in a glebe, but it is open to all of us to live, walk, work and play in God's love.

We can take our own glebe with us!

Friday – February 2

PEOPLE have lived atop Carn Brea in Cornwall since the Stone Age. Since the Ice Age, the hill has been topped by a pile of gigantic granite boulders – the sort it might take explosives or a bulldozer to shift.

When, in the 14th century, the locals wanted to build a chapel on that spot, they didn't move the boulders. They used them as the firmest of foundations and built the chapel on top of them.

How will you deal with the obstacles in your path today?

Saturday – February 3

THERE'S a statue of a man in London's Canary Wharf. He is stocky, rough-hewn, his arms are spread wide and his head is tilted towards the sky.

He "speaks" to me every time I see him. I don't know if I see him as me at my best or at my worst, but I do recognise that stance. A little leaden, but essentially joyful, and giving thanks!

Sunday – February 4

THOUGH time and tide might separate
And miles lie in between,
Yet thoughts can travel far away
Of all we've done and seen.
Some memories are safely stored
And some can never die,
Reminding us, just one more time,
How quickly years go by.
So keep the love and joy we've known,
A treasure all life long.
Whatever life may have in store
This love will keep us strong!

Iris Hesselden

Monday – February 5

IN her novel, "Three Apples Fell From The Sky", Narine Abgaryan explains the names of several fictional Armenian villagers who lived through World War I.

One is named after her promise to pay back a debt, one is named after the foreign wife he brought home, one for her complexion, one for the type of hat he wore, and so on.

Imagine if we each had a name other than our given one – an earned one.

If we were called after a personality trait, or the impact we had on the community, would we like it? If not, might we learn to live our lives in such a way that we earned a name we would love?

Tuesday – February 6

MELANIE works as a street pastor, which means night shifts at the weekends.

She tells me that, at about four a.m., she takes herself to the brow of a hill where she can see the city spread out in front of her.

There she appreciates all those people sleeping safely in their beds. Then she goes home, but never without reminding herself why she does what she does.

Take time to give thanks – even when you would rather be in bed.

Wednesday – February 7

WATCHED an old video of Pavarotti singing with Bono. The Edge and Brian Eno played the music, along with the orchestra behind them, and thousands of people watched some of the most famous artists in the world perform as images played out on a massive screen.

Pavarotti was every inch the world-class tenor, dressed in a fine tuxedo and doing what he loved. A music stand, with what seemed like a sheet of marble on it, was positioned in front of him.

The lyrics to the song were on that marble sheet (or whatever it was), held in place by two wooden clothes pegs!

The whole performance might have been ruined if they hadn't done their job!

Even among the grand and the noble, do not disparage the little things.

Thursday – February 8

DESPITE some serious learning difficulties, he helped out at the community café every week.

The first time I met him, I walked him to the bus stop after his shift, because someone was set on robbing him.

The second time, we talked – in peace – about his love of S Club 7 and his love for his mum.

The third time was more awkward, because there was nothing new to say about S Club 7, so we talked some more about his mum.

The fourth time, he took my hand as we crossed the road to the bus stop.

Friday – February 9

IT'S a line credited to the actress Sandra Bullock. "The rule is, you have to dance a little in the morning before you leave the house, because it changes the way you walk out in the world."

I don't know if the Oscar winner said it or not, but it makes sense to me, and I am so tempted to try it!

Start the day off right with a little joyful dance.

Shutterstock.

Saturday – February 10

AT this time of year, rain is probably more common than sunshine. On an "interesting" day, we might have both!

Edward Thomas was a writer who died towards the end of World War I, but in more peaceful times he was commissioned to write a history of Oxford, and in that book he referred to such days.

"The rain and sun alternating are like two lovers in dialogue".

I don't suppose it makes any difference practically to think of such days in that way, but it makes unpredictable weather a lot more romantic.

Sunday – February 11

THERE'S a lot of friendly – and some not so friendly – rivalry between various science-fiction fan bases, in the same way that there is rivalry between different football teams, religions and nationalities.

"The New York Times" poked fun at that, and also might have shown a possible solution to it in – of all places – its crossword puzzle!

The clue was "The better of two sci-fi franchises".

The answer, which fitted perfectly among the other answers, changing some, but still leaving them correct, was "Star Wars" – or "Star Trek"!

The best way to resolve any dispute? To make sure that both sides win.

Monday – February 12

THE world owes a debt to Charles Darwin, but his work on species and evolution came at a cost.

He regretted that his mind had become a machine for grinding laws out of facts.

His ability to appreciate art, poetry and music seemed to have disappeared along the way, and he was sure it was to his detriment.

On his birthday, and on his behalf, let's give equal time, if we can, to the science of life and to the beauty of it all.

Tuesday – February 13

HE said hello in such a way that I stopped and prepared to apologise for forgetting his name. I was sure we must have been old friends, but he had walked on. We'd never met.

It reminded me of a man I met years before, who smiled at me in a way that convinced me I had never truly been smiled at before.

"Guileless" is the word. Without deceit, expectation or ulterior motive. It's a beautiful thing to experience, and is a wonderful thing to share.

Wednesday – February 14

FROM that very first smile
Which appeared on your face;
From that tentative touch
To the full, warm embrace;
From the moment I knew
What my heart was now feeling,
To this Valentine's Day
Where my love I'm revealing.
You're the love of my life as you were from the start,
And from then till for ever you'll be in my heart.

John Darley

Thursday – February 15

RUSSIAN novelist Alekandr Solzhenitsyn, writing in "The Gulag Archipelago", argued that the line between good and evil does not run between states, parties or even individuals.

Instead, he suggested that it ran through the hearts of each of us – and that it was moveable.

We might be more to one side than the other at different points in our lives, but we don't have to stay there.

Given that he might have been right, when better to work on moving that line in the right direction than today, a day dedicated around the world to random acts of kindness?

Be kind to someone for no reason today – and any other day. The other person will reap the benefit of your kindness, but so will you!

The arrival of snowdrops heralds the coming of spring.

Friday – February 16

THERE'S an old Scottish expression I love: "We're all Jock Tamson's bairns". It means we're all children of the same family, equal and loved, no matter our race, creed, or colour.

There is no definitive answer as to the origin of the phrase.

Some credit it to a minister, John Thomson, who used to urge the congregation closer to the pulpit by shouting, "Gather round, ma bairnies!"

Whether we believe in a Creator Father or biology, we don't need to look back many generations to discover relatives in common.

Biology and faith – both tell us we are family. We might as well behave like it.

Saturday – February 17

SOFT and still, their silent bells hang down
'Neath the frosted sun of shortened days.
Only they can prove our hope is sound –
Winter cannot keep the spring at bay.
Drops of white caught in a snowy ring
Reborn from that which slumbered underground.
Oh, blessed are we by all the joy they bring,
Peering out, just waiting to be found.

Laura Tapper

Sunday – February 18

HANS CHRISTIAN ANDERSEN told a story in which he met a puppeteer on a river boat. The puppeteer told of a convivial evening he had spent with a physics lecturer.

Both were fascinated by each other's talent, but the puppeteer thought he had the best of the discussion, because so much of what the lecturer shared was a mystery to both of them.

The lecturer, rather than being affronted by this, agreed.

"The whole world," he explained, "is but a series of miracles. We are so accustomed to them that we call them ordinary."

I don't believe the great Danish storyteller ever looked at anything and thought it ordinary!

Monday – February 19

GRAN and Grampa were trying to get a two-year-old to nap. Grampa lay down on the couch, apparently to set a good example.

Just then, Gran realised the little boy's favourite toy, Chew-bear, was missing.

"Oh, dear," Grampa remarked, fearing there might be tears. "What shall we do?"

The little boy looked at him for a moment.

"I be Chew-bear," he said, then tucked himself under Grampa's arm.

"It just melted me," Grampa admitted to me afterwards. "He didn't have his own comforter, so he became a comfort to someone else. Me!"

It reminded me of an old saying:

"Where there is no love, put love – and there you will find love."

Tuesday – February 20

I HAVE seen an uplifting variety of Little Free Libraries in different locations around the world.

The idea is that you take a book for free when you see one you like, then you leave another book for free that someone else might like.

The simple idea has generosity and appreciation written all through it.

Well, yesterday I thought I saw such a library – a roofed box, with two shelves, on a short pole.

But there were no books. The sign said "Take a rock – give a rock".

At first I thought it was ridiculous.

Then I thought back to my childhood and the pockets I wore out by carrying favourite stones around.

Stones and rocks have stories to tell, just like books.

Learning to appreciate such humble things will, no doubt, put us back in touch with those early days – when everything was amazing and worth sharing.

Wednesday – February 21

CLAUDE MONET, whose painting of the gardens at Giverny earned world-wide acclaim, is supposed to have credited his becoming a painter to flowers.

If you like who you are, give credit where it's due. If you don't, then why not find a more beautiful inspiration, then paint a fresh picture?

Thursday – February 22

I'VE hugged a tree, planted a tree and admired many a tree, but I don't think I've ever made friends with one.

Then I talked with others about how Henry David Thoreau, the American writer and philosopher, would walk 10 miles through snow to "keep an appointment" with a yellow birch, a beech and a pine tree he thought of as old acquaintances.

A surprising number said they had favourite trees, too. They had never set out specifically to visit them, but they thought Thoreau's idea was a jolly good one!

Far be it from me to suggest that trees wouldn't make good friends. In fact, the more of each of those, the merrier!

Friday – February 23

JOHN EVERETT MILLAIS'S painting "The Blind Girl" depicts two sisters sitting in a field. The elder one is blind, and has a concertina on her lap. She busks for her living, but at least she has music.

The younger girl is half-hiding under her sister's shawl, peeking out at a double rainbow. Meanwhile, the elder sister warms her face in the sun and rubs grass between her fingers.

Birds sit nearby, a stream runs behind them, and no doubt she hears them both. A butterfly rests on her shawl. The sign on her breast says, *Pity the blind.*

But who are the real blind? One girl seems only too aware of the beauty around her, while the other hides away.

In a world where there is so much beauty, like the rainbow, the sound of the stream, the warmth of the sun, or that butterfly, I do pity those who can't find any of it.

Saturday – February 24

I HAVE heard that "in the Irish" a person never says they are sad. They say, "Tá brón orm", meaning "the sadness is upon me".

It's a wonderful reminder that we are more than our feelings.

Sadness, or any other emotion, is not who we are, so let's not define ourselves so narrowly. We are more than any one emotion.

The feelings, good or bad, will come and visit for a while – then they leave.

We will be who we always were – essentially wonderful.

Sunday – February 25

IT'S a little redemption story. Not about a person, though. The big table was probably due for the rubbish tip after decades in an office environment.

Pastor Nathan was converting part of the church's balcony into an office space. The table was free for collection, so he picked it up.

Now that old table sits in sunlight for most of the day, basking in the colours of the stained-glass window above it, while sermons of love are written on it.

You never know how things will turn out, do you?

Monday – February 26

SOMETIMES it seems an effort just to brush and comb your hair.
If you don't put on your lipstick, will people even care?
But the person at the bus stop, who smiles and says hello,
Is pleased to see you out today; your presence makes them glow.
That you took the time to make it there, looking bright and breezy,
Just being where you're meant to be has made life a bit more easy.
Your quiet words of welcome have sent them on their way,
Lifting up their spirit high, to help them face the day.
Never think you're not important in the grand scale of events,
Or question why on to this earthly planet you were sent,
Because, indeed, the truth is that you're part of God's great plan
That binds us all together – a brotherhood of man.

Elizabeth McGinty

Never underestimate the difference you make in the lives of others.

Tuesday – February 27

THE Roman poet Horace, who lived in the first century BC, experienced his fair share of ups and downs in life, and learned much from them.

In his "Odes", he advised an unhappy friend to "set limits" on his sadness, noting that the south wind, which so often brought showers, just as often cleared the clouds away.

A difficult thing to do when we are feeling down, but always a wise thing to remember.

Wednesday – February 28

FIFTY years ago, five young girls got together and decided they would meet every fortnight for sewing and chat.

The original five are three now, with some new friends for company, and the sewing bee still goes on.

Those young girls have been mothers, grandmothers and great-grans. They've patched clothes in hard times, stitched garments for each other's wedding trousseaus and knitted baby clothes for generations of babies.

Some folk might think it a little fanciful to celebrate a sewing bee's birthday, but 50 years of friendship is an achievement well worth celebrating, if you ask me.

Thursday – February 29

IN the 1900s, Art Young was a cartoonist and political activist. He worked for women's suffrage and the abolition of child labour.

In 1927 he published a collection of drawings called "Trees At Night". His skill lay in giving twilight silhouettes human characteristics.

My favourite is one of the rare ones that includes a human figure.

The tree is leaning over and in danger of falling. The man holds it up with one hand, and gives the roots a drink from a watering can held in the other hand. It's called "Hope".

Doesn't that sum up so much of what life is about? Accepting it isn't perfect, but doing everything we can to make it better.

March

Friday – March 1

A POLARISED society is, sadly, nothing new.
Almost one hundred years ago, in his "Homilies And Recreations", the Scottish novelist John Buchan wrote about a literary community divided between the old and the new.

While defending his own traditionalist stance, he also understood that the modernists were the future.

"Both sides," he wrote, "defend a truth which is not all of the truth."

An absolute victory of one side over the other would only serve to destroy part of the truth.

Worth reminding myself of, I think, the next time I insist on being right.

Saturday – March 2

WHENEVER I find myself diverted by the things of the world, I'll glance at a photo held on our fridge by a magnetic souvenir.

I took it in the summer. It shows a narrow, rectangular flower-pot. Its sole reason for existence is to decorate the entrance to a pub-diner.

It sits between the building and the car park, so there are cars and humans passing by most of the day.

There are two bees in that picture. I watched them for 20 minutes while waiting for someone. None of the man-made stuff, none of the hustle and bustle, distracted them at all.

All they cared about were the flowers in that box, and pollen-collecting was their sole focus. No matter what!

It was a balm to my soul.

When the fuss and fury of the world becomes overwhelming, remember your purpose, remember why you are in this world, and stick with that!

Sunday – March 3

*M*EMORIES *are such precious things,*
As to the mind each one can bring
Fond images of yesteryear,
Laughter, joy, perhaps a tear.
Who would have thought, way back then,
They'd bring comfort again and again?

Pamela Ramage

Monday – March 4

NOTICED our local am-dram director repeating a simple instruction to his players: "Eyebrows up!"

"It's an old theatrical trick," he explained afterwards. "It makes the character seem more in the moment.

"And it does help keep them there!" he added.

I tried it myself afterwards.

It increased my field of vision, making me more aware.

It actually did make me feel like something was about to happen, so I made things happen and became more productive – for a little while.

We do get into lazy habits, though, don't we? And anything that shakes us out of them has to be good.

So, eyebrows up!

Tuesday – March 5

WAS done in when I got home," Harry told me. "But my dog still loved me.

"I had a day when I was less than I might have been with someone, and my dog still loved me. I came home in a bad mood, and my dog still loved me!"

"Your dog must think that you are pretty wonderful," I suggested.

"Aye," he agreed with just a hint of a smile. "But I'll think I'm wonderful when I learn to love the way she does!"

Wednesday – March 6

THE Lady Of The House and I marvelled at the church's combined charity shop and food bank.

Once a small house, every corridor, room and cupboard was full of donations.

They were filled with things that had been used in the small community, and could be used again. And food!

"You could find everything you needed here, if you looked long enough," my sweetheart remarked.

I asked one of the volunteers about the nameplate on a door.

It had been painted over so many times that the engraving was barely legible.

"Oh, that's the name of the church officer in the 1950s," she explained. "This used to be his house.

"I sometimes wonder what he would think if he saw it now," she added.

I've no doubt he was a fine man who would never have imagined his home being used in this way, but the poor were being clothed and the hungry were being fed.

I am sure that raised a smile in heaven.

Thursday – March 7

IT was an inscription on a memorial bench in a country park.
It read: *For some people, small beautiful events are what life is all about.*

How true!

I didn't know the couple whose names were inscribed there, but I am sure I would have liked them!

Friday – March 8

THE fourteenth Dalai Lama said, "Choose to be optimistic. It feels better."

The great shifts in our approach to life can be made for such simplistic reasons.

Saturday – March 9

THE advice is so old now that I doubt anyone really knows who was the first person to say it.

But I believe that it holds true today, and it is always worth repeating.

A guru once told a seeker of wisdom these words:

"Before enlightenment, chop wood and carry water. After enlightenment, chop wood and carry water."

The point being made here isn't that enlightenment will make no difference to your life.

The point actually being made is that, once you can fully appreciate them, the most ordinary things in your life will seem like blessings.

Plus, if you have both firewood and water, you will have the makings of a hot bath from which to contemplate the universe!

Sunday – March 10

A FANCIFUL legend suggests that Simnel cake – associated with Mothering Sunday – was first made by a couple called Simon and Nell.

They couldn't agree whether the cake should be boiled or baked, so they did both.

They should have asked their mothers!

Share a cake, some flowers or a nice day out with your mother today, and thank her for all the special, and ordinary, days she arranged for you.

Monday – March 11

WARREN is always acquiring things that he believes he can do up, then sell on for a profit.

So much so that, before a recent trip to the local dump, his wife Theresa warned him against bringing back more than he took away.

It reminded me of the advice I was given long ago, to "fix more than you break and give more than you take".

*I WONDERED what to talk about;
I wondered what to say!
Except "It's nice to see you. Nice!
Let's have a happy day."
It's time to have some cheerful thoughts
And time to raise a smile,
To put aside the troubled world
For just a little while.
To look at all the growing things
And watch the birds and bees,
To see the beauty in the sky
And in the waving trees.
So if you don't know what to say
Or words are hard to find,
Let nature's gifts inspire you
And lift your heart and mind.*

Iris Hesselden

Wednesday – March 13

A FRIEND'S father, in her younger years, encouraged her to write letters of complaint, should she feel the need.

She was to leave them under her pillow overnight, and if she still felt it was worth sending them in the morning, she should do so.

Legend has it that Abraham Lincoln would write angry letters, then walk across the Oval Office and burn them in the coal fire.

A more artistic friend would save his grievances for a carefully timed walk along the shore.

He would write them in the sand with a stick, just above the waterline, as the tide was coming in.

I have, I admit, written many an annoyed e-mail, then pressed *Delete* rather than *Send*.

Sometimes, we just need to get it out, to feel we had our say, rather than end or damage a relationship.

Some complaints should still be sent, of course, but the morning after a good night's sleep would seem to be the very best time to send those.

Thursday – March 14

THE book, from the Fifties, had a "Missions to Seafarers" sticker on the cover.

It urged the crew to swap the books donated by the mission with other seamen, wherever they might be.

A friend, who sailed in a tanker in the Seventies, said they used to do likewise with movie reels.

"You were always guaranteed something interesting," he told me. "If you were lucky, it was in English."

Sharing good things around the world? It's a beautiful idea.

Might we set up a "mission" to do the same in our neighbourhood, or amongst the people we meet?

Friday – March 15

OUR dear friend Mary was smiling when I met her in the street. "I love seeing people who have no idea how wonderful they are," she said. "Going about their business and unconsciously making the world a nicer place as they pass by."

"Who was that? I asked, looking around.

"You don't know?" she asked. "Well, then, perhaps it was you!"

I doubted it. I'd just left the house. Was it you?

Saturday – March 16

I WATCHED a child, playing with small toys, completely lose herself in an imaginary world.

It was incredibly frustrating for the mother who was trying to get her organised.

But, as a viewer, not involved in the organising, I saw a child who didn't have to leave a part of herself on guard, a child not involved in the necessities, the fear or distractions of life.

Because she was loved, and she was cared for, she could immerse herself in play without a second thought.

Not every child in this world has that luxury. It was a beautiful thing to see.

A sense of safety and comfort opens the door to imagination and joy!

SPRING comes
With its own fresh breath,
A celebration
Voiced in song,
Resurrecting
Life from death,
A force of nature,
Vital, strong.

This season
With its great unrest
Is from confinement
Now unfurled;
Both sky and earth
Are coalesced
As colour floods
Into its world.

John Darley

ROY ROGERS, known as the "King Of The Cowboys" in Hollywood during the 1940s and 1950s, also became a father to a little girl born with Down's syndrome in 1950.

She was the only biological daughter of Roy and his wife, Dale Evans Rogers.

Robin Elizabeth died of complications associated with mumps just before her second birthday.

Her mother wrote about the little girl's life in a book called "Angel Unaware".

The book was written as a report to God by an angel returning to heaven, and it told of the lessons that her mother and father had learned in loving and losing her.

It is a heart-breaking story, of course.

But it did make me wonder how I would fare in the final reports of those who – in need of help or otherwise – crossed my path in this life.

Tuesday – March 19

MOST of us are familiar with images of Egyptian pyramids. They are simply and elegantly constructed, and meant to last for ever.

But did you know that, during the reign of the pharaoh Sneferu, two pyramids were built that seem to have been the Egyptians figuring out that classic, lasting shape.

The first prototype partially collapsed "in antiquity".

The pyramids seem always to have been perfect. And some people give the same impression.

We see their successes, but rarely see the trying and failing process that led them there.

Don't set out for perfection, and don't give up when you don't achieve it.

Set out to try, set out to learn, set out to improve.

The Egyptians got there. So will you!

Wednesday – March 20

STOPPING at Chester Cathedral in 1874, a young Robert Louis Stevenson found some choristers at practice.

The verger, seeing him appreciating their singing, spoke to him.

"Ah, you're very fond of music. I could tell that by your head. There's a deal in that head!"

Stevenson's father interrupted to say his son had no ear for music.

Upset by this, the verger sought out the elder Stevenson later that day to protest.

He was comforted to learn that Robert Louis Stevenson's "great deal" found an outlet in literature.

The verger and the father's contrasting attitudes reflect the approach some adults give to a child's creativity – some will shut it down, and some will encourage it.

It is my opinion that each one of us is born creative – somehow.

To express that creativity, we need two things: to discover our passion, and not to have it quashed.

Thursday – March 21

IN his poem "The More Loving One", W.H. Auden talked about the stars, and how he loved them even though they didn't know he existed.

"If equal affection cannot be," he wrote, "let the more loving one be me."

No doubt the stars were metaphors for lopsided human relationships.

And one partner loving more than another in a relationship can lead to all sorts of problems.

But if we take it as a personal challenge, as how we might be in relation to the rest of the world, then it becomes so much more positive and uplifting.

On today, World Poetry Day, we might spend a little time appreciating the works, and learning from the thoughts, of the world's poets.

Friday – March 22

IF you have a car and children, then you have probably felt like a taxi driver at one time or another.

For a parent, running the children here, there and everywhere is all part of the job.

It is a small price to pay for the freedom that a car brings, and the delight of having children – but we like to complain, even if it is just in jest!

I thought of all this one day, when I looked in the window of a parked car.

I saw a pretty, embroidered, rectangular cushion on the driver's seat.

It was perfect for lumbar support, and stitched across it in flowery script and bright colours were the words:

Thank you, Mum, for all the lovely things you do!

I thought, there's a mum who must feel appreciated wherever she goes.

And at least one child who is getting driven to wherever they want to go!

Driving children is part of the job for a much-appreciated parent!

Saturday – March 23

PEOPLE who claim they are a self-made man or woman always make me wonder.

Did no-one hold their hand while they learned to walk? Did no-one help them work through difficult homework? Did no-one cook them hot meals or keep a roof over their heads?

Perhaps the care given – or not given – was such that they would rather not acknowledge it. Which is a shame.

Really, none of us is completely self-made. Perhaps we should stop using the phrase as a badge of honour, and get back to where we ought to be, which is helping each other make it in this life!

Sunday – March 24

THE family had already climbed several flights of steep stairs from the seaside cove. Having reached the top of the cliff, there was still a winding, rising path to the picnic site.

The six-year-old girl decided her legs were falling off and she needed carried.

The nine-year-old boy proclaimed that the only way he was going to get there was on his daddy's shoulders.

Just as it looked like there might be tears, Grandad sprinted through from the rear.

"You're not going to let an old man beat you to the top, are you?" he shouted, and both children took off like rockets.

It just proves the old saying: "If you think you can't, or if you think you can – you'll be right!"

Monday – March 25

IS heaven a place we hope to go to after we die? Or is it a reborn Earth, due to be transformed after the Second Coming?

Of course, no-one really knows.

Until we get a definitive answer, let me offer this advice by Jack Kerouac, the great American novelist. In a poem, written at the end of a letter, he said, "Practise kindness all day to everybody, and you will realise you're already in heaven now."

Tuesday – March 26

THEY say that, in the Persian language, the expression for being poor translates as "my wings are tied."

While that might sound like a fairly desperate situation, it implies it was a situation outwith our control that caused the current situation, and we might yet get those wings free again.

Better times, clearer skies and higher flights await!

Wednesday – March 27

HE looked about twelve years old, following his mother around the supermarket as if it were the last thing he wanted to do.

He walked after her, engrossed in his phone.

When she turned from one set of shelves to the other, she found him standing there, with his head bowed – so she kissed it!

Of course, he objected, embarrassed, but his mother just laughed.

"That's a mother's love for you. You need to watch out for it, or it'll get you."

Mother love – it surprises all of us. Even, I am sure, the mothers themselves.

Thursday – March 28

TWO brothers, one six and one four, were on holiday in a house in the woods.

They were set for adventure, but the four-year-old couldn't seem to get 20 yards from the house without turning back to add another pine cone to his collection.

The exasperated six-year-old was frustrated.

"They're pine cones," he told him. "You don't need any more. They're all the same!"

Then the four-year-old explained in great detail how each pine cone in his collection was unique.

One had been chewed by squirrels, one looked like a rose, one had tiny green leaves growing from it, and so on.

I can't wait to see how he collects his friends!

Find the strength to rise above the things holding you down!

Christ of the Abyss, San Fruttuoso, Italy.

MATT, who James had been at school with, went "off the rails" and ended up in jail.

Hearing Matt was out again, James decided to pray for him.

More, he decided to teach him about faith and help him get his life back in gear.

They started meeting up. It was strange at first, but he persevered.

"I think I helped him," James told me. "Having someone believe in him made a difference. But he helped me more. I learned so much about him, about the world, and about myself!"

James stumbled upon an under-appreciated aspect of the life of faith. Doing the right thing often isn't easy. Attempting it can be a journey of exploration through our fears and needs.

We grow as people by helping people. Perhaps that's the real point.

Saturday – March 30

HOW are you feeling?" the Lady Of The House asked.

"A bit bored. This awful weather isn't helping my mood any!"

"Good, good!" she replied happily, so I asked her why.

"If the day's spoiled already, you can do some of those jobs you put off doing in case they spoiled a good day."

I did remember saying such things, so I grudgingly set to work.

To be honest, I didn't appreciate her wisdom, but I did get a lot done!

Sunday – March 31

SEVENTEEN metres down in the Mediterranean Sea, off the coast of Italy, stands a bronze statue of Jesus. It's called Christ of the Abyss. His hands are raised towards the surface and the sun.

The sculptor, Guido Galletti, meant it to portray that moment when Christ rose from the abyss of death on Easter morning.

This Easter, may we think about all the worldly things that hold us down, that make us less than the children of faith we ought to be. And may we find the strength to rise!

April

THERE'S a Philosopher's Walk in Kyoto, Japan, named for the great Japanese philosopher Nishida Kitarō, who would walk that way to Kyoto University, where he was a professor.

I hear there's one in Königsberg in Germany, where Immanuel Kant used to stride out. Heidelberg has another.

Aristotle called his academy in Athens a Peripatetic school, because he found he did his best thinking while walking.

And the Ancient Romans had a saying, "Solvitur ambulando", which means, "It is solved by walking".

Now the weather is picking up a bit, why not get into the habit of a regular walk? I can't promise it will make you a great philosopher, but it might help you think a few things through.

Even if it only makes you fitter, that's no bad thing, either.

Let's be philosophical about it!

Tuesday – April 2

IN 1938, Douglas Corrigan bought a second-hand plane and fitted it with an engine he built himself. His plan was to fly across the Atlantic, but the Bureau of Air Commerce only certified it over land.

Filing a flight plan from New York to California, Corrigan took off.

Then, claiming to mis-read his compass in heavy clouds, he flew the wrong way – to Dublin!

For ever after he was known as Wrong Way Corrigan, but the parade held for him on his return attracted more people than the Charles Lindbergh parade to celebrate the first solo transatlantic flight.

The people who do things differently will often be labelled "wrong way" by society. The question we should ask is: does their way make the world a better place?

Wednesday – April 3

HE was a little the worse for drink, and he was having an animated discussion with the shopping centre security guard.

It seemed that the guard had helped someone and not been thanked.

"And, and, and . . ." The man struggled with his indignation. "You keep them safe all day and they walk right past you! They don't have eti . . . etiquette to say thank you!"

The guard just shrugged.

I thought about it afterwards.

The guard is employed to do those things. Like so many people whose job is to quietly make things easier and safer for us.

What would it cost us to notice them and say thank you?

Nothing at all, but it would make their day better.

Thursday – April 4

I WAS reading a farmer's account of taking corn to market in the 1840s.

The market was on Saturday, so they loaded the cart on Friday evening, covering it, then securing it.

But before they put one thing on the cart, they made sure it was standing on "good ground", so it would move with its load in the morning.

Standing on good ground was important then – and it still is.

Friday – April 5

MY winter heart is lifting, as dreams of spring abound,
Tulips tipped in sunshine, a crocus carpet ground,
A panoply of pansies will display their violet hues,
And doubled-headed daffodils will also pay their dues,
Snowdrops will spread gently, and their fragile heads will rise
As hyacinths bring splendour, lilies reach for the skies,
Primroses preen proudly and irises stand tall;
A floral feast of colour as spring now comes to call.

Karen Stokes

Saturday – April 6

HE'D heard it was a habit of Himalayan porters. He used it himself on a work trip, when he stayed in several European hotels over the space of three weeks.

I use it on particularly busy days.

The porters asked for regular stops on their treks to allow their souls to catch up with their bodies.

When my friend left one hotel for another, he would pack early, then sit in the lobby for 10 minutes, appreciating the rest the hotel had offered.

And I like to find a few minutes after each task, just to say, "That worked out well."

Never be too busy that your soul loses track of you, or that you have no time to be thankful!

Sunday – April 7

MANDY stood on the shore in the middle of a bay. After a busy but happy day, she'd taken a bit of time to think and watch the sunset.

At each end of the bay, churches of different denominations raised their spires. The moon sat in the sky above one, and a near vertical section of rainbow hung above the other.

Moonlight and rainbows – two expressions of the same source, she realised. Very different, but reflecting the same light in their own particular ways. Just like the churches.

Monday – April 8

I THINK it's a tribute that originated among the aboriginal population in Australia. When a good man or woman died, they said that they walked gently upon the earth, meaning that they passed this way and did no damage.

Of course, people considerate enough to do no damage also tend to leave things better in their wake.

Walk gently upon the earth and among its inhabitants. She is our mother, after all, and they are our family.

Tuesday – April 9

OUR dear friend Mary had been to tea with a particularly prickly character; someone I usually like to avoid.

"I'll never understand why she has to say things like that," I protested at one point.

"I don't try to understand," Mary told me. "I see the unpleasant stuff, but assume there is more to her and love her anyway. I try to overstand."

Overstanding rather than understanding. I like the sound of that.

I'll give it a go. For Mary, and the good there might just be in it.

Wednesday – April 10

MICHAEL was a man who always had to be right. Then he was disciplined at work for something he did wrong.

"There were mitigating circumstances," he told me, "but I messed up. It made me feel sick."

When he told his wife this, she said, "Every time you have insisted on being right, you've probably made the person in the wrong feel just like that."

"I've changed my approach since then," he told me. "Now I remember the old maxim, 'If you need to choose between being kind and being right, choose being kind – and you'll be right'."

Thursday – April 11

WHEN all at once I saw a crowd, A host, of golden daffodils." Most of us will recognise this line from William Wordsworth's immortal poem "Daffodils". They conjure up an idyllic picture.

But according to Dorothy Wordsworth, who was there on the day, one friend had quit their Lake District walk due to the weather. The morning was "threatening" and "misty", and the wind "furious".

A far from idyllic day. But perhaps these things made the simple daffodils – being buffeted by the wind, but preserved by the rocks they grew amongst – all the more enchanting.

If your day seems difficult, stride out regardless. Who knows what wonders and beauties you will see that meeker souls might never?

Friday – April 12

IT was entertaining, listening to the two-year-old boy chatter. One thing struck me. Every time he talked about "my daddy", he spoke like a child who loved and admired his daddy.

It brought a lump to my throat.

I knew the boy's father had a distant relationship with the grandfather, who used the callous behaviour of the great-grandfather to justify his lack of emotional availability.

It seems – wonderfully – that this "Daddy" has managed to break that cycle.

"Mummy" and "Daddy" should always be words spoken with love. It isn't always so, which makes it all the more heartwarming when we hear them spoken properly.

Saturday – April 13

THE Lady Of The House and I were discussing the idea that, in friendships, talking is important, but listening is more important.

"It just occurred to me," my sweetheart said. "Our mouths are made so they can open and close.

"Our ears are actually designed to stay open. If only we used them that way, friendships might last longer and grow stronger."

And I can relay this spontaneous wisdom to you because – smug husband that I am – I was listening!

Sunday – April 14

IT'S a simple line, written by the poet William Cowper to the Reverend William Bull in 1792.

Having mentioned the difficulties of their journey and talked about those he sorely missed, Cowper added, "But soon after this latest separation, my troubles gushed from my eyes, and then I was better."

Ah! The healing powers of a good "greet", as they say in some parts.

May God bless all who shed genuine tears, and may God be thanked for the good they do us!

Monday – April 15

THERE'S a story of a workman hired to paint a small sailing dinghy. As he painted, he noticed a hole in the hull.

Because he could, he repaired the hole, then finished the painting.

Two days later his employer gave him a cheque.

He protested it was too much for the paint job. It was even too much for the painting and the repair!

His employed explained.

"I knew about the hole, but I'd forgotten to get it fixed. The day after you painted it, my children took the boat out, assuming it was sea-worthy. If you hadn't done that repair for me, I might have lost them."

The workman took the cheque and pondered – as we all should – on how we never really know all the good we do when we do a good thing.

Tuesday – April 16

IT would be a sad thing to get through a life never having loved. It would be a rare thing to get through a life never having loved and lost.

Travelling south from Abbotsford in 1828, the great Scottish novelist Sir Walter Scott wrote that his arrivals in Carlisle were sad occasions.

It was there that he had married his recently deceased wife, Charlotte. And there he could not help thinking of her.

Scott had proposed to Charlotte after a mere three-week courtship, and then married her despite his parents' concerns about her background.

It was a true love match in a time when that was not always the socially acceptable thing to do.

"It is something to have lived and loved," he wrote.

"And our poor children are so hopeful and affectionate that it chastens the sadness attending the thoughts of our separation."

Few lives are without loss and sadness.

May we endeavour to live in such a way that the things that outlast us will be suitably – happily – chastening to our sorrows.

Being generous in our appraisal of others can bring out their best.

Shutterstock.

MANY of the paintings left by J.M.W. Turner look misty, hazy and out of focus, which has led to speculation about his eyesight.

In 1849, a Mrs Simon recalled an encounter with the artist for his supporter John Ruskin.

She told Ruskin she was startled by Turner's eyes.

They made her think of her grandfather, of whom it was said his gaze "could make a hundred ugly faces handsome".

Turner had, she said, "The most seeing eyes I had ever seen."

I have no insider knowledge about the great painter; no explanation.

Perhaps a lifetime of looking for beauty will do that to us. If not always to our eyes, then at least to our souls.

Thursday – April 18

ONE of my favourite Beatles stories concerns the recording of "Because" for the album "Abbey Road".

A slow piece, it required precise time-keeping from everyone.

Despite there being no drums on the track, Ringo Starr played a precise beat away from the microphone, which the others could hear through headphones.

He helped make the track, but never appeared on it.

That's what friends do. They build others up without seeking credit for themselves. All the more reason to sing their praises !

Friday – April 19

I HAVE heard the advice offered (in less enlightened times) to wives about their husbands, but that wasn't its original purpose!

In the novel "Handley Cross" by Robert Smith Surtees, Spooney worries he hasn't bought the best of horses.

He is advised he will get the best from his new mount if he is "to his faults a little blind" and "to his virtues ever kind".

It's advice that will bring out the best in whoever – or whatever – you apply it to.

Saturday – April 20

I LOOK up to the mountains whenever I feel low,
Trusting God is with me and will never let me go.
I see the sunlight sweep across slopes reaching to the sky,
Pointing out the way to him, who hears the heart's deep cry.

The traffic roars, but still I hear the birdsong clear and true,
Above me, clouds are clearing and behind them skies are blue.
There are people on the cycle path chatting cheerfully,
Their voices rise upon the air, laughter ringing free.

I look up to the mountains, made by his mighty hand,
Their majestic, silent witness visible across the land.
My Father can do anything, these peaks spell hope to me –
There's no such word in heaven as impossibility.

Marian Cleworth

Sunday – April 21

HELEN KELLER, the American author and activist, is supposed to have said, "So much has been given to me. I have not time to ponder over that which has been denied."

Two of the things denied her were hearing and sight.

Even so, she felt her life's blessings outweighed its shortcomings.

The next time we feel the urge to complain, let's take a minute to thank God for the good things in our lives.

Then, if we still offer up our complaint, it will hopefully be done in a more appreciative way.

Monday – April 22

JOHN MUIR was the Scotsman who helped set up the United States National Park system.

I do like this description attributed to him of the benefits of being outdoors.

"Nature's peace will flow into you as sunshine flows into trees. The winds will blow their own freshness into you, and the storms their energy, while cares will drop off like falling leaves."

Tuesday – April 23

DOING some garden work, Harry uncovered an 1893 Victorian half-penny.

"I looked it up," he told me. "It's really not worth much unless it's in mint condition. But this one was worn, like it had been through many pockets, tills and purses.

"A deep score ran across it, and I wondered if it had been made by a spade, plough or blade. I tried to remember the history of the land and guess whether a farmer or a traveller had lost it.

"If it had been preserved straight from the mint, it would have been story-less. We're all born in mint condition," he continued. "But life marks and shapes us.

"That's what makes us unique; that's what gives us our worth. So I'll keep the ha'penny until I lose it in my turn.

"It's worth more to me for having 'lived'."

I looked for a moment at Harry and considered the ways life had marked and shaped him, and wholeheartedly agreed!

Wednesday – April 24

I FOUND it in an archive of historic photos. And it stayed with me. It was a picture of a young girl, taken in the 1930s, during the Great Depression in America.

She – bless her – is smiling for the camera, while looking off to one side, presumably to her mother.

She wears shoes that look too big for her, perhaps borrowed for the occasion.

Her legs, from knee to ankle, look freshly washed, in contrast with other parts of her.

But as captivating as she and my hopes for her were, my attention was drawn to the wall behind her.

It had been "decorated" with pasted-on sheets of newspaper.

One of her parents had hung an extra sheet of newspaper so it hung over the window, pelmet style, and they had cut the hanging end in a pretty scalloped design.

Human beings! There is no state of poverty they might find themselves in that they will not try to make more beautiful!

Thursday – April 25

MICHAEL AISLABIE DENHAM was a merchant and collector of folklore. In the 1850s, he published a collection of rhymes, prophecies and proverbs from the Durham area.

In it, he talked about the new fashion of walking for recreation.

"It is customary for these walkers, as they are called, to enter a house without knocking and take a seat by the fire. Some still retain the good custom of keeping a bed for the walker."

Providing shelter for travellers is a custom as old as society.

We might not live in a world where people can just walk into our houses and sit by the fire any more, but we could and should find new ways to be hospitable.

Hospitality should always be at the heart of who we are.

Friday – April 26

WHEN Joan of Arc was being tried by her captors, they asked questions she thought none of their business, like details of her visions and of her private life.

Often they would be traps for her to incriminate herself.

To those questions, she would respond, *"Passez outre"*, by which she meant "Move along", or "Next question, please".

In other words, she wasn't going to answer. Even in captivity, she retained enough dignity to know that.

The approach reminds me of the modern saying, "You don't have to attend every argument you are invited to."

When you get such an invitation, feel free to reply, *"Passez outre, s'il vous plait!"*, or "Move along, please."

Saturday – April 27

WHICH is more important," the seeker after enlightenment is said to have asked his teacher. "The journey or the destination?"

"Each has great value," the master replied. "But the most important thing is the company."

Can I humbly suggest that how we leave the company feeling at the end of the journey might be just as important?

Sunday – April 28

IT'S a phrase that has been used by two Popes and accredited to at least two saints.

Whoever said it, the version passed down to us today translates as, "See everything, overlook a great deal, fix a little."

Whether we are overseeing vast organisations or dealing with family disputes, it stands as good – and peace-keeping – advice.

Know what's going on, avoid the stuff that leads to unnecessary arguments, and fix something.

If you stick with that advice, after a while you will have fixed a lot – and everyone will still be talking to you!

Monday – April 29

I WAS embarrassed to be taking my books back late, so I threw myself on the mercy of the librarian.

"By keeping books out," she told me, "you do us a favour."

I looked confused.

"The library actually has more books than it has shelf space for," she explained. "If everyone brought their books back at once, we would be in trouble!"

The thought stayed with me. A heart should put more love out into the world than it could ever hold. Lived properly, a life should put more help into the world than it receives.

We and the library benefit from our partnership. We and the world, likewise!

Tuesday – April 30

IN a conversation with a younger friend, Theophilus, novelist John Buchan said he found much of modern poetry "cacophonous".

"Your ear has grown dull," Theophilus said. "Anybody who has got accustomed to the Popian couplet would have felt the same thing about Blake and Shelley. We are making new tunes, and in fifty years the world will have grown accustomed to these, too."

Appreciate what went before, because what is old now was once a new tune.

May

FATHER, hear the prayer I pray:
Give me courage every day.
Send your love and healing, too,
For everything I have to do.
When the future's looking bleak,
Let me find the hope I seek.
Wrap me safely in your care
And show me you are always there.

Iris Hesselden

POPPED into a pub for some lunch. Across the aisle from my table, three young men shared a booth.

They'd had enough to drink that the conversation was descending into nonsense. They weren't careful about the language they used, either, but were always polite and respectful to the waiting staff.

Then the conversation died down.

I was focused on my lunch, but I heard a lament being sung, too quietly for me to make out the words.

When the song finished, I turned around. They were sitting with their heads bowed, but gradually realised I was looking over.

"Who was singing?" I asked.

"Ah, I think that was me. Sorry," one of them replied.

"That was beautiful!" I told him, and you should have seen them smile!

It would have been easy to dismiss them as immature, as annoying, or as boys who drank too much, but who would have known there was so much beauty in both in the singer and in the appreciation of his friends?

The youth of today, eh?

Friday – May 3

IN my time, I have had music on "the cloud", in MP3 format, on CDs, cassettes, LPs, 45s and even 78s.

I don't quite date as far back as wax cylinders, though.

But music goes a lot further back than that. Did you know that the earliest piece of written music – the "Hurrian Hymn No. 6" – dates to 1400 BC?

Each generation tends to despair of the music of the next generation, but the truth is, music has been with us almost for ever.

It serves no practical purpose, but we are never without it.

It's a thought that not everything in the world serves a necessary purpose.

Some things – like that tune you were humming earlier – are there simply to enhance the experience of living!

Saturday – May 4

DO you ever hesitate to approach others because of what they might think?

Did it ever occur to you that they might feel the same?

Most people, I find, appreciate the effort it takes.

The poet Emily Dickinson understood.

She explained why she thought it was worthwhile in her poem "They Might Not Need Me – Yet They Might –".

She wrote: "A smile as small as mine might be Precisely their necessity."

Sunday – May 5

IT was listed as "A Prayer Found In Chester Cathedral" (1770). In it, the writer asked for some ordinary but important things: good digestion, a healthy mind, a sense of humour – and the ability to see sin without being appalled, "but find a way to set it right."

Often what we see as sin is made worse by our reaction to it.

Let us not be the ones who turn away.

Music can really enhance our world.

Monday – May 6

AUTHOR and screenwriter Ray Bradbury was one of the most creative minds of his generation.

Whether his stories were set on Mars, in a dystopian future, or in small-town America; whether they were sci-fi, horror, or set in the ordinary world, he imbued them with a realism that came from being a keen student of human nature.

His books have lived on my shelves many times, but my favourite words of his were reportedly spoken during an interview.

"Looking back over a lifetime, you see that love was the answer to everything."

Obvious, isn't it? But it often takes a special way of looking at the world to see something that evident.

Tuesday – May 7

AMERICAN novelist Kurt Vonnegut once wrote a poem about an experience he shared with Joseph Heller, the author of "Catch-22".

In it, he told how they were both at a party thrown by a billionaire. Everything there was way over the top.

Vonnegut asked Heller how he felt about the fact that their host made more money in one day than "Catch-22" (a hugely successful book) ever made.

Heller was unfazed by the question. He replied that he was OK with the idea, because he had something the billionaire didn't.

"What's that?" Vonnegut asked.

"Enough," Heller replied.

Wednesday – May 8

MODERN ceilidhs tend to be organised events, with music and dancing. Originally, the word meant "company" or "visit". The visitors would contribute a song or a story in return for hospitality.

In other words, they would be good company.

Things are different these days, but if you have a story to tell or a song to sing, you can take the ceilidh with you, wherever you go!

Thursday – May 9

LONG before garden slabs were so easy to buy, my gran used the ashes from her coal fire to make the path to, and around, her drying green.

When they first went down, the path was lumpy and crunchy, but they eventually made a good, smooth surface that was excellent at keeping the weeds down.

If ever any of us children complained of having nothing to do, she would suggest a walk around the drying green.

"If you've nothing better to do," she would tell us, "you might as well make the path a better one for us old and infirm folk."

She wasn't old or infirm back then – just appealing to our youth and vigour, giving us an excuse to go stamping.

But her advice stayed with me.

If ever I have a difficult path – real or metaphorical – to walk in life, I try to leave it a little smoother for the next person.

Friday – May 10

ONCE clocks have changed, a carpet soon appears
In ancient woodlands, in between the trees:
Bells of violet-blue, with tiny curlicues,
Which dance and shiver gently in the breeze.

The scent of such a multitude of blooms
Weaves a fragrant primaveral spell,
Amid the insects' hum, dappled by the sun,
This surely is the realm where fairies dwell.

Gone the darkling haunts of nymphs and fauns
Made young and fresh again, decked out in blue.
Alas, it cannot last; they fade and wither fast,
All things have but a season, it is true.

So tiptoe lightly when you come to call,
Sure to leave the flowers where they be –
A precious gift to share, of worth beyond compare,
Such treasure must remain for all to see.

Laura Tapper

Saturday – May 11

JULIE'S eight-year-old daughter had just spent the day out and about with her grandparents.

Returning home, she looked exhausted, but it was still light and she still wanted to go out and play with her friends.

"I told her she didn't look like she had enough energy to play with friends," Julie explained. "She told me, 'My friends give me energy!'

"It left me wondering which of my friends gave me energy, and which I might do that for – and glad she had such lovely friends!"

Sunday – May 12

I'VE heard it said that most church-goers' favourite hymns and translations of the Bible will be the songs their grandparents sang and the Bible their grandparents used.

In other words, the ones they grew up with.

I once asked my neighbour, Harry, which translation of the good book he liked the best.

"My granny's," he told me.

So I asked which translation his granny had used.

"I have no idea," he confessed. "But I did love the way she translated it into everyday life!"

Monday – May 13

IN Nepal, they use the greeting "Namaste", which means something like "I bow to the divine in you".

Zulus have the word "sawubona", which means "I see you, and you are important to me".

Don't greetings like that make our "Hello, how are you?" seem a little boring?

Well, only if you don't mean it! The Nepalese and Zulu greetings would sound just as mundane if the person using them wasn't all that interested.

When you say hello to someone, remember there's no-one else like them in the world. Greet them like you care, no matter what language you use!

Time with friends can replenish your energy.

SHEILA'S two-year-old grandson was in his car seat, directly behind her as she drove.

After a few minutes of silence, she heard him say, "Ooof!"

"What was that?" she asked, and he replied, "I back!"

"Oh?" she said. "Where were you?"

"I fly over the sun," he replied. "Now I back!"

Imagination is one of the best parts of being a child. If we grow out of it, it's a bit like being grounded.

Wednesday – May 15

PEOPLE who comment on society sometimes make our differences seem like obstacles. They don't need to be.

In his book "Country Boy", published in 1966, Richard Hillyer talked about how different he and his brother were.

"We were two people, as different as could be in our ways and our thoughts, yet each perfectly accepting the other. He would listen to my confidences without understanding them . . . just taking them as coming from me and no doubt making sense so far as I was concerned.

"Not treating them as trivial because they were not his own, listening to them patiently but making little comment, and taking them just as they were part of me.

"He had his ways and I had mine, neither could be the other, but we were sure of each other, that was what mattered."

Very different, but very close. It is possible!

Thursday – May 16

WHEN poet Robert Lee Sharpe was a boy, he went with his father to the blacksmith's shop to pick up a repaired rake and hoe.

His father offered payment and the blacksmith refused. Father insisted, and the smith replied, "Can't you let an old man do something now and then, just to stretch his soul?"

Acts of kindness – the best way to enlarge a soul!

Friday – May 17

THERE are two "equal and eternal" ways of looking at the world, the writer G.K. Chesterton insisted.

"We may see it as the twilight of the evening, or the twilight of morning. We may think of anything, down to a fallen acorn, as a descendant or an ancestor."

Are we, he asks, a young and experimental species, or are we nothing more than the inheritors of a glorious past?

An old story coming to an end, or a new story beginning? The wonder of this world and our lives is that something is always finishing and something is always springing to life.

Both sides of the equation are equally true. Which side seems the dominant one might depend on our circumstances.

We might be a glass half full or a glass half empty type of person, but the fact is that the glass is constantly emptying, and constantly being refilled.

Should we be sad about the world, or happy? Personally, I think we should be amazed!

Saturday – May 18

A FARMING friend told me about clearing the rocks from a ploughed field (in the good old days).

It was an onerous chore, but one that had to be done yearly to keep that patch of ground green and productive.

Often, as he wrestled them from the dirt, it would become obvious that the stones were scarred from previous contacts with the plough blade.

How like the petty dislikes and prejudices that many of us hide just under the surface, I thought.

These hidden "rocks" bear scars from contacts with people or places that might have improved us as a whole, if we hadn't knocked them aside.

The farmer might dread clearing away the stones, but he knows the end result will be worth the effort.

Likewise, if we could join him in carrying a few of our own personal "rocks" to his trailer for disposal, we, too, could look forward to experiencing the green shoots of new growth.

Sunday – May 19

SAT in silence and heard nothing. I tried again the next day and heard a seagull.

On the third attempt, I heard the traffic on a distant road.

I could tell a truck from a motor bike. I heard our water boiler. I heard our neighbour's dogs.

Where were all those things the first time I tried? They'd been there, but I was so used to hearing them that I tuned them out.

Intentional, prayerful silence works like that.

We might try the first time and hear nothing, but . . .

Monday – May 20

IN Robert Louis Stevenson's poem "Where Go The Boats?", a little boy contemplates the river and wonders where the floating toys that leave his hands end up.

Eventually, he decides that other boys would – even though they were a hundred miles away – bring them to the shore.

Reading it, I couldn't help but wonder if Stevenson was thinking about the good we put into the world: the kindnesses that seem to have no immediate effect, but bless someone else further down the river.

Tuesday – May 21

JAMIE had a Facebook friend request from someone he didn't think he knew, until they mentioned clothes poles.

The year before the COVID pandemic, this person had house-sat for his neighbour for a week. Hanging out the washing on the first morning, they couldn't find a clothes pole.

When Jamie saw the clean washing dangling in the neighbour's foliage, he passed one of his clothes poles over the fence – and that was it!

All these years later, after the other person had been out the country and returned, the kind deed was remembered.

People say the small things are important. I'd say, they are so important that, when it comes to kindness, there are no small things!

Our kindnesses can travel
"down the river" so to speak!

Wednesday – May 22

THERE'S God among the daffodils and Jesus with the weeds;
The Holy Spirit in the earth encouraging the seeds.
Look! Joseph's clearing up the pond; Eve's singing to the bees;
Queen Esther, dizzy with the scents, is hugging all the trees.
St Michael finds the slugs some shade; Ruth mends a blackbird's nest;
Some cherubs check out butterflies – they're definitely impressed.
The seedlings grow, the plants bear fruit, the ants work, rain or fair;
Come harvest-time, there's food enough for everyone to share.
I'd never manage by myself; I'm helped the whole year through.
This garden may be mine, but it's a piece of heaven, too.

Ewan Smith

Thursday – May 23

IN Ontario, Canada, there's a museum dedicated to failures! It displays a range of products and services that were offered by some famous companies around the world, but proved to be commercial flops.

Products like New Coke, the DeLorean car and Google glasses.

The point isn't to poke fun at them, although I am sure a few, perhaps nostalgic, laughs are had by visitors. The point is to show that innovation is a minefield, and for every product that becomes a commercial success, a huge number of products will be left behind.

It's the same in our personal lives. We won't always succeed, but we need to keep trying.

If the ways we try outnumber the ways we fail, progress will have been made!

Friday – May 24

I COULDN'T say who the Lady Of The House was talking to on the telephone, but something of the conversation might be understood by this snippet of advice she offered.

"Set yourself small challenges. Things you can achieve. Those little things will add up to a big difference."

IN 1950, Irish writer Frank O'Connor produced a short story called "The Idealist". The main character was Delaney, an Irish schoolboy who read stories set in English public schools.

He wished he attended such a fine "old pile" and mixed with such "grand chaps".

The "chaps" of the stories were adventurous, exciting and shared a high moral standard.

His own school, he decided, was not at all like that. Comparing the two, he decided the problem wasn't the school buildings, and it wasn't the money or the resources available to the students.

"What was really wrong," Delaney decided, "was ourselves."

He decided to hold himself to the higher standard depicted in the books – and it all goes wrong.

I'll depart from the story here to say, whether the stories were realistic or not, it does all come back to us.

If we see a better world somewhere, fictional or not, and we feel that's the way our lives ought to be, then it's up to us to make them so.

We might not change the whole world (or the whole school), but we will change our corner of it!

Sunday – May 26

THE brilliant sun of early morn,
That blinding light as day is born,
Golden yellow, intense delight,
Now dawn has rolled away dark night.
I stand in awe of a wondrous scene
'Neath a sky of blue in fields of green;
I feel the radiance warm my face
As the sun arises, serene the pace.
I realise now why ancient man
Worshipped the sun as bare he ran
Across the earth as down it shone
And hid in caves when it was gone.
But now we know it's God, through you,
Gives life to all, blest orb so true.

George Hughes

Monday – May 27

AN old tale speaks of a competition between two lumberjacks. They set out to see who could cut down the most trees in a day.

Both men powered through the morning, then, come lunchtime, one stopped for a break.

Seeing a chance to pull ahead, the other lumberjack kept chopping. By mid afternoon, his energy began to fade away.

The man who stopped seemed renewed and won the competition.

"I chopped for longer and still lost!" the one man wailed. "You stopped! Surely having your lunch didn't make all that difference."

"Lunch helped," the winner explained. "But after lunch I sharpened my axe."

Working smarter will always beat working longer.

Tuesday – May 28

I SAW Roger on his way home, fishing basket slung over his shoulder and rod in hand.

"Catch anything?" I enquired.

"No." He showed me the basket. "But I caught some memories of fishing with Dad. I caught the breeze in the reeds, some sun, and a lot of peace!"

Wednesday – May 29

THERE are many stories from the filming of David Lean's cinematic masterpiece "Lawrence Of Arabia". Some are true, some are a bit more showbiz!

One such story concerns a scene where the actor Peter O'Toole had to lead a charge, mounted on a camel.

Apparently he was so scared he had a few stiff drinks beforehand – then fell off the camel, into the path of some galloping horses!

But the camel he'd been riding stepped over him and stood there, saving him from harm.

It might not be a true story, but it reminds us that our fears often turn out to be other than what we expected. Sometimes our fear is actually more damaging than what we were afraid of!

FERDINAND CHEVAL built a palace in France. Was he a king? A billionaire? A conqueror? No – he was a postman.

He started building Le Palais Ideal in 1879 and it took him 30 years to complete.

The palace is a mix of styles. It has a spiral staircase, a Swiss chalet, temples of different faiths and statues of giant human figures.

It is 26 metres long, 10 metres high, and is now preserved by the state.

Every stone and rock that went into its construction was collected by Cheval on his postal routes.

After a while he resorted to taking a wheelbarrow along with him, but for years he would carry the stones in his pockets or his mail sack.

The very first stone he used was one he tripped over and then put in his pocket.

How's that for turning a stumble into progress, an obstacle into an achievement?

SOME time in the early 18th century, Sir Richard Steele wrote in "The Tatler" of visiting a married friend.

The husband suggests that Steele, a bachelor, must have noticed that his wife wasn't the beautiful woman she'd been when they first met. Steele protests that the husband cannot expect his wife to be for ever a teenager.

The husband insists that Steele has misunderstood. He explains that the "fading in her countenance" was mostly caused by caring for him when he was ill.

Other lines occurred while raising their family and running the house.

"There is no decay in any feature which I cannot trace to some anxious concern for my welfare and interests."

Because of that, the differences in her appearance only increased his love for her. A life well lived will take its toll on anyone's features. A few of us are lucky enough to be able to read the stories preserved there.

June

AMY and Ryan's two-year-old son, Oran, has wakened up in the wee hours twice in the past week. Both times he was really upset.

The first time, he wanted to know if his stone collection was OK.

The second time, he was in tears at the thought they might have run out of blueberries.

How do we respond? We might laugh afterwards. But at the time, faced with his obvious distress, his parents chose to assure the little lad that his stones were fine and the blueberries were plentiful.

We might be older, but are we so much wiser when it comes to the things that are important to us?

Perhaps, when we are relating to others in our "grown-up" world, we might judge their priorities less by how important we think they are, and more by how important they are to them.

THERE'S beauty in nature, in everything,
From the buzz of the bee to the flap of a wing,
From the old fallen tree in the woods by the trail
Brought down by the weather in another winter gale.
The clumps of bright dandelions dotting the path,
The wren in the puddle, taking a bath,
The nettles a home for the large cabbage white,
The weeds in my garden looking a fright,
The moss on the wall in a carpet of green,
The ivy that clambers and twists in a screen
Up the bark of the old gnarled sycamore tree
That has seen so many more seasons than me.
Yes, this is my place, where I take time to be
At one with myself, just nature and me.

Diane Inglis

Monday – June 3

JUNE, according to Sara Coleridge, the daughter of poet Samuel Taylor Coleridge, "brings tulips, lilies, roses" and "fills children's hands with posies."

Doesn't that sound sweet? Perhaps a little old-fashioned?

I don't know. Take a child to a wildflower meadow, or any place where flowers as allowed to grow free, and watch them.

You'll see. As long as there are children, and as long as there are flowers, I think Sara Coleridge's poetic imagery will remain true.

Tuesday – June 4

BACK in the 1920s, the writer J.B. Priestley was having a grey day, in a grey week, when he walked past a clothes shop and saw some scarlet silk pyjamas in the window.

Such a purchase would have clashed with everything in his wardrobe and everything in his lifestyle, but life was getting very monochrome, society bowing to uniformity.

So he bought those exotic pyjamas, saying there were times "in a man's existence when he must make something happen, must fling a splash of colour into his life, or some part of him, perhaps the boy in him, will perish."

If the little boy or the little girl in you could have their way for a while today, what sort of splash would they make?

Wednesday – June 5

IT was quite apparent that the young busker was blind. She stood in the flow of pedestrians, sang "What A Wonderful World" and collected loose change.

Anyone familiar with the song will know it contains a list of beautiful things – "trees of green, red roses, too", "skies of blue, and clouds of white. The bright blessed day, the dark sacred night" – which she would never see.

Do I think she chose that song deliberately to tug on heartstrings?

I do. Do I think the message of appreciation was any less relevant and important? I do not.

Children will find the magic and joy in a field of flowers.

Thursday – June 6

ALMOST a decade ago, on a bus, I overheard two men discussing addiction.

One had managed to get free, while the other was still in the grip of whatever drug it was.

"Take help," the first man urged him. "It's like being in quicksand. If you struggle by yourself, you sink. But someone standing on solid ground can help pull you out."

Ten years later, those words still come to mind in many different situations.

Don't struggle by yourself. Take help!

Friday – June 7

HOW would you like to overcome all the troubles in the world? The legendary American folk singer Woody Guthrie is credited with saying, "There ain't but two things in the world can cause trouble. One is greed. The other one is fear. There ain't but one remedy for both, and that is love and friendship."

Maybe our love and friendship won't save the whole world, but if we each take care of our little corner . . .

Saturday – June 8

HARRY was passing on some tools he doesn't use any more. First, he wanted to make sure they were in working order.

"Some of the pliers and grips were rusted shut," he told me. "But some oil loosened them up.

"Then there was the twelve-inch shifting spanner. It's probably the oldest tool I own. Maybe forty years old. Every time I pick it up, it just works! That went back in the tool shed."

I reflected on the fact that I had known Harry for the same length of time.

That spanner was a metaphor for a certain type of friendship – properly made, neglected at times, but still works just fine when needed.

I'm just glad Harry doesn't keep me in the tool shed!

Sunday – June 9

CRAIG is the money man at our church. I have never met anyone with a head for accounts like he has.

All our social programmes owe him huge thanks.

He took me along to a meeting with some charitable funders.

When they offered him more than he expected, he said, "Excuse me. I'd just like a quick word with my boss."

He nodded at me and we left the room.

Out in the corridor, he held a hand up to ward off my questions, closed his eyes, and said, "Lord. If you want us to do this . . ."

You might have plenty of money, and all the success you need, but never forget who the boss really is.

Monday – June 10

THEY were written in Latin in "The Thoughts Of The Emperor Marcus Aurelius Antoninus".

I have heard them preached from a pulpit.

My own grandmother said them to me (hoping I would understand) when I had fallen short.

It matters not where they come from, or who speaks them – words of wisdom are words of wisdom.

What were they?

"If it is not right, do not do it. If it is not true, do not say it."

Tuesday – June 11

THERE'S an old story of a man living in an isolated croft whose family persuaded him to accept his first TV.

A week or so later, they asked him what he thought of this "new innovation".

"Weel . . ." He sighed. "I've been watching it quite a bit, but I think I've had enough. I haven't seen a freen or neebour yet!"

Television can be great fun, but you can't beat face-to-face contact with the people you know – or those you might get to know!

Wednesday – June 12

THERE'S a story the Scottish writer and author of "Peter Pan", J.M. Barrie, is supposed to have told.

It concerned a young monk who lived in a monastery surrounded by fields.

One summer day, his duties completed, he went for a walk.

While walking, the monk (Anselm was his name) saw a lark take flight. He stopped and listened, enraptured, as the bird seemingly sang its way up to heaven.

Eventually, deciding the day wouldn't get much better than that, he turned and walked back to the monastery.

When he arrived, he recognised no-one there. And no-one there recognised him.

After much confusion, the records were checked and it seemed that a Brother Anselm had, indeed, lived there, but he had disappeared a hundred years ago.

There are moments when beauty, wonder or the joy of life just wrap us up and time seems to stand still. Perhaps not for as long as Anselm, but clocks definitely have no place in moments like those.

I do hope you know them!

Thursday – June 13

WHEN physicians are measuring recovery, they might refer to decreases on the pain scale, or increased angles of flexibility.

Harry measured his recovery from sciatica very differently.

"At its worst, I was sleeping on the couch. Or, rather, not sleeping on the couch. Then it improved enough that I could lie on our bed – but only on one side, and facing away from my darling.

"Eventually, I could turn around without too much pain, but only for a few minutes. After that, we could cuddle for a while before I had to turn back to the pain-free side.

"But that little while got longer and longer. And last night, for the first time in a month, we slept the whole night in each other's arms."

Recovery measured by how long you can cuddle. I can't wait for the medical profession to adopt that scale!

Friday – June 14

FRANCIS GAY has loved libraries since they were places of reading and shushing.

The local library of my childhood has long been demolished. There have been years of financial cuts, closures and difficulties.

My new local library (the one after the one after the one I first went to) is a place of books, but very little shushing.

It also has LEGO for children, a chess club, basic education classes, a film club and a "Worries Chair" – if you sit in it, someone will come and talk to you.

Today there was a plate of fairy cakes, baked by one library user for other library users.

Francis Gay loved the libraries of a different era. He loves the modern ones even more!

Saturday – June 15

JANE is a painter, a quilter and a writer, and she works part-time.

When I asked her how she fitted everything into the time she had, she agreed it wasn't easy, but said, "I practise these little arts for the sake of the one big art – my life!"

I'll ask you the same question that inspired in me. How is your masterpiece coming along?

Sunday – June 16

SOMETIMES," the minister told me, "a sermon falls flat! Having tea afterwards, the congregation will talk about the weather, the latest news – anything but the sermon. I've had that happen often enough, but I don't despair.

"Because – months later – someone will tell me how it seemed God was talking to them that morning, how they took the message away, and the difference it made!

"And, for every person who tells me, I'm convinced there will be others who don't!

"When I'm up there talking, I don't know who needs to hear what I'm saying – but God always does!"

Modern libraries provide wonderful community hubs.

Monday – June 17

IT'S a nonsense tale with an important point. Two frogs fell into a half-filled milk churn. Seeing no way out, one frog quickly gave in and sank. The other frog kicked and kicked, and kept kicking.

Eventually, the milk turned to butter and the frog jumped out.

The frog could never have imagined such a transformation would occur. And the same thing happens when we keep trying.

Opportunities we could never have imagined at the beginning will almost certainly appear – if only we don't give up!

Tuesday – June 18

AS boys, they were cousins and friends. Separated by only a few days between their birthdays, they had a special bond.

But families moved, life got in the way and half a century passed.

Then Tom met Danny's brother, and heard that Danny had made some unfortunate choices, straying from the straight and narrow. No-one had seen him for a while.

Out of childhood loyalty, Tom sought Danny out and they arranged to meet.

But Tom worried. They were men now. There would probably be all sorts of barriers up. This might be a one-off before they separated again, perhaps for ever.

But as they stood, a handshake's distance apart, Danny said, "Remember when we were young enough to hug?"

And that was the beginning!

Wednesday – June 19

SOMETIMES it seems like there's a "World Day Of" or an "International Day Of" everything under the sun.

I do enjoy World Sauntering Day. In fact, I enjoy it on as many days as I can.

A saunter, a stroll, is a carefree thing. And if you aren't carefree at the start of it, your load of cares will surely be lighter at the end.

Slow down. See more of what there is to appreciate in the world. Your soul will thank you!

Thursday – June 20

IT'S one of those jokes that depend on national stereotypes – but there's more to it.

An Englishman and a Scotsman were travelling in India.

They reached a spot where there was a particularly wonderful view of the mountains.

Knowing the Scotsman was proud of the hills of his homeland, the Englishman said, "The Himalayas are so tall!"

"Aye," the Scotsman agreed. "But only the tops of them."

He was obviously prepared to be impressed by heights he'd never reached in his native Highlands, but wasn't giving an inch as to the quality of the heights he was familiar with.

His devotion was with the burns, the corries, the glens, the crags and bens he knew so very well.

We might be like that with people at times. Someone might be known to be "high and mighty", but we have no idea what they love, what they miss, how they are when they are tired or hungry.

Heights might rightly and fairly be admired, but it's a wise idea to familiarise ourselves with the foundations on which they stand.

Friday – June 21

THE foodbank was getting a bad reputation. According to gossip, the wrong people were getting free food; some were even selling the packages on. There was a worry that people might stop donating if they thought their efforts were being frittered away.

I told the stories to the administrator. He smiled and said he'd heard them.

"What are you going to do?" I asked.

"Nothing," he replied. "People were always going to take advantage of that. Should I tighten the rules to keep them out and, maybe, shut out someone in need? I'd rather not."

The love in that mindset was, I thought, wonderful. And we can take it into our own lives.

If someone takes advantage of our good nature, who do we help by making our nature less good? No-one. Not even ourselves.

Stay loving.

Saturday – June 22

BEFORE the sermon, the minister asked, "If you were to learn a new thing, what would it be?"

People said they would like to learn a new language, learn to drive, learn to swim, and so on.

But one woman said something a bit different.

"I'd like to learn something new about everyone in this church, so we could all grow closer by it."

The sermon was well received, but the minister left the church with a new mission. One he would recommend to us all.

Sunday – June 23

CREATE a work of art from the unmaking of your bed,
Or maybe make your millions on the stock exchange instead.
Some might favour politics, a game of truth and lies,
But if you're prepared to study, quizzing offers quite a prize.
From what the papers say, a novel's worth a bob or two –
Why not write a book for children; that's a wizard thing to do!
Pick the perfect numbers and the balls might go your way,
Or Ernie could decide it really is your lucky day.
But for what you have, be thankful, there's no point in selfish greed,
The best things are so often free, how much do we truly need?

Laura Tapper

Monday – June 24

THE textbook, published in 1921, was issued by a girls' boarding school. It contains selected essays from the "King's Treasuries Of Literature".

But the inner covers have newspaper cuttings pasted all over them.

The cuttings are reports of football matches between various ladies' teams. No doubt they were "hidden" there by a young fan in the year the Football Association banned women's football from its grounds.

"Treasuries", it seems, can come in many unexpected guises.

Tuesday – June 25

I'VE been revisiting some favourite nursery rhymes with a young friend recently.

I rather like the thought in the last verse of "Mary Had A Little Lamb". It suggests that it was her love that made the lamb follow Mary in and out of school.

It continues: "And you each gentle animal in confidence may bind, and make them follow at your call, if you are always kind."

I don't know about gentle animals, but I'm pretty sure it would work with gentle people.

Wednesday – June 26

THE local wise man was tired of people coming to him with the same old problems.

Therefore, every time a villager visited with a complaint, he told them a joke.

It was a funny joke, and people laughed. The first time.

The second time, they laughed less. The third time, they wondered if he was losing his memory. Then they came out and asked him about it.

"You don't like to hear a funny thing over and over," he said. "But you will complain about the same unhappy things for ever."

There is something in us that likes to complain, and something that is less fond of finding solutions. That's no joke!

Thursday – June 27

THE shopkeeper had, apparently, been in pain for some time. "It's left me hobbling about for a fortnight," she told her customer. "I look out of the window and see people walking without even thinking about it. It could happen to any of them. They have no idea what it's like!"

The woman next in line (in front of me) leaned forward and said, "This is my first pain-free day in a year, and it's wonderful! You have no idea what that's like – yet. But you will!"

Actually, both were right!

A SMALL hand in mine on a long summer trek,
A kingfisher, spied darting over a beck,
The woods, filled with bluebells, in calm, dappled sun,
The bread in the oven which smells almost done;
A bench, with a view reaching over the bay,
A card from a friend, who lives so far away,
Your welcoming face, and that warm cup of tea –
Just some of God's blessings, which help sustain me.

Chris Young

Saturday – June 29

THERE were things on her mind, so Julie didn't sleep well. She felt awful the next morning.

The next night, she had her ten-week-old grandson overnight to give Mum a break.

That meant that she was up every four hours, feeding and changing the little one. She spent quite a bit of time gazing at him in the low lamplight. The end result was that she got even less sleep.

The next morning, she felt great! What made the difference?

"What you do in love," Julie told me, "always feels great."

Sunday – June 30

SHE had attended the church for years. Then her mother died. No-one from the ministry visited her.

A few years later, her father died. It was the same again.

Shortly afterwards, she left the church.

There were other problems, of course. Meetings were called to investigate the situation. Questions were asked and polite answers were given. A strategy was devised.

She heard most of this second hand, because she was already gone.

We can have as many committee meetings as we like. We can devise endless strategies. But they will avail nothing if we do not obey that clearest of Christ's commandments, and love one another.

July

IN his mind, he was following a trail through the jungle. In reality, he was a two-year-old boy in the communal garden outside his home. He stopped in front of a little cloud of what I called "flies".

"No," he told me in all seriousness. "They is gnats!"

"Are they, now?" I asked. "Who told you about gnats?"

"Nobody," he replied. "I just knowed."

No-one's born knowing about these beasties. Someone had, at one time, named them for him, but he thought he'd always known that.

All too often we are shaped by people and events we forget, but the impression they make on us, or the information they impart, stays. And we think it is just us.

If only we gave credit where it was due for the good stuff that shapes us, leaving behind the negative stuff we think is us – but never actually was!

Tuesday – July 2

I WINCED in sympathy. A new family had recently moved into the neighbourhood and, not having a handy-man among them, Harry was building their plastic and metal garden storage hut.

Stopping by briefly, sure he would benefit from my supervision, I listened a while. Behind the windows, three generations were yelling their needs, complaints, demands and excuses.

All the while, Harry worked on. Quietly.

"I hope they are paying you well," I told him.

"I'm just being a good neighbour," he replied. "Besides, which do you think would do more good for the world, a little more money in my pocket, or a little more grace in their lives?"

I've heard of the labourer being worthy of his hire, but Harry is the first workman I have ever met who measures his wages in terms of what's best for the world.

Wednesday – July 3

HAVE you ever made a mistake? Ever wished for a "do-over"? Louisa Fletcher, who lived at the turn of the 20th century, knew the feeling.

In her poem "The Land Of Beginning Again" she wrote:

"I wish that there were some wonderful place called the land of Beginning Again,
Where all our mistakes and all our heartaches and all of our poor selfish grief
Could be dropped like a shabby old coat at the door, and never put on again."

The good news is that there is such a place! The Land of Beginning Again is tomorrow! Each bright new day is a chance to start afresh.

Thursday – July 4

HE told me his addiction was self-medication for anger caused by childhood abuse. He insisted that he wasn't nearly as angry these days. But I could see that anger peeking through his son's eyes.

Now he's a different man, clean for years, having gone through talking therapy. I reserved judgement until I saw his son, and when I did I saw a happy young man, loving life with his dad.

On US Independence Day, I am reminded that freeing ourselves doesn't only set us free.

Friday – July 5

LUDWIG VAN BEETHOVEN was one of the most famous people who ever lived. His life had equal shares of happiness and tragedy.

Of all the things he experienced, which do you think would have made him the happiest? Composing music? That's what I would have thought. It's certainly what he is known for around the world.

But no. Anton Schindler, one of the earliest of Beethoven's biographers, recalled seeing a scrap of paper on which the great composer had written, "Love, and love alone, is capable of giving thee a happier life."

Music is wonderful. But nothing beats love!

Every new day is
an opportunity
to start afresh!

Saturday – July 6

THE little girl stopped before the life-sized portrait of a ballerina. She did her best to adopt the same pose, then laughed out loud as she lost her balance and fell over.

Undeterred, she tried again and again, loving every minute of it.

I looked around at the other, more serious, museum-goers, and recalled the advice the writer J.B. Priestley offered to people in another museum – advice that could be applied to so many other things.

"Stop tip-toeing! Have some fun! Find some delight in this place . . . or march straight out!"

Sunday – July 7

LITTLE Aaron is about five years old. The youth pastor asked him and some other children on to the stage to help with an action-filled praise song. Many of the grown-ups stood up and joined in.

I was surprised by how well one as young – and as shy – as Aaron did with all those different actions.

Then I discovered his secret. He was watching his mum. His actions were mirroring hers.

It was an insight into how powerful the examples we set are. Our children watch us and learn from what they see.

Which makes it so much more important that we set positive examples in our lives, our actions and our faith.

Monday – July 8

THE Ancient Greek philosopher Democritus said, "Happiness resides not in possessions and not in gold, happiness dwells in the soul."

The Roman emperor and thinker Marcus Aurelius said, "Very little is needed to make a happy life; it is all within yourself."

Richard Wagner, the German composer, said, "Joy is not in things; it is in us."

It's a truth that perseveres across the centuries. Even if you have nothing else – be happy.

Tuesday – July 9

OH, wasn't that awful!"
A young friend was listening to the story of an older friend's "illegitimate" birth.

The older friend remembered her mother saying that, while she was in labour, she was offered a selection of rings to choose from before being admitted to the ward, so it wouldn't be obvious to everyone that she was pregnant while being unmarried.

"How awful that there was such stigma!" our young friend exclaimed.

Absolutely.

But how kind that someone sought to alleviate that stigma for her!

Wednesday – July 10

IT'S not often I am annoyed with our dear friend Mary, but she called me recently to ask if I had any tissues.

What? Did she want me to walk round to her house with tissues just because she had a sniffle? Couldn't she go to the shop?

It turned out that she was getting ready for a funeral, where she would be in charge of two little girls grieving their grandmother. Hence the tissues.

That strange request suddenly seemed like the most caring and thoughtful thing I had heard in years. We judge too quickly, sometimes.

Like I said, it's not often I am annoyed with our dear friend Mary. And when I am – I'm usually wrong!

Thursday – July 11

I WALKED one way through the shopping precinct. No-one spoke to me.

I walked back again and tripped over an uneven surface. I fell on to my hands and knees and five people rushed to help me. One woman wouldn't let me go without asking if I was all right five times – I was.

People aren't as cold as we are sometimes led to believe. They just need a chance to show their warmth.

Friday – July 12

MARGARET BARBER, who wrote the Christian classic "The Roadmender" under the pseudonym Michael Fairless, also wrote a short piece in praise of rivers.

She described one river where she used to daydream in a boat, another that was a companion in contemplation, a brook she used to explore as a child, a stream bounded by beautiful flowers, and even the muddy old Thames, where countless ships were being unloaded.

Each of them spoke to her in different ways at different times, but always to the benefit of her soul and her peace of mind.

If you can, get acquainted with a river and go with the flow for a while. You'll be glad you did.

Saturday – July 13

HAVE you ever wondered why people graffiti walls, or why they choose to vandalise? It's an easy way to make a mark or to be noticed. Easy, but destructive.

Her Majesty Queen Elizabeth II, in her 1957 Christmas broadcast, said, "It has always been easy to hate and destroy. To build and to cherish is much more difficult."

Anything worth anything in this life will take a bit of work. Whether it be our words, attitudes or behaviours, don't take the easy way out.

Put in the effort to make sure they leave a positive impression on the world.

Sunday – July 14

IN his poem "Raiders' Dawn", the Welsh poet Alun Lewis referred to two lovers who fall victim to war.

In his diary he called the same lovers "the seed of humanity", which, he insisted, would outlive war. He declared that life was "normally and perpetually a miracle".

Love will outlast war, and life is miraculous. When the going gets tough, those thoughts will make it all worthwhile.

The message in the Gospels will tell you how to put them into everyday action.

Make a positive
impact on the world!

Shutterstock.

Monday – July 15

WHEN two-year-old Oran travels by car, he usually takes "PAW Patrol" or Buzz Lightyear toys along to play with.

On longer journeys, there is often a tablet to watch cartoons on.

This day, however, was a less organised one for his mum.

Along the path to the car park, they realised they hadn't brought anything to keep him occupied. Mum expected tears, but Oran picked up three stones that just happened to be lying there.

For the entire journey, those stones had adventures while he kept up a running dialogue between them.

What a blessing a healthy imagination is!

Tuesday – July 16

HARRY has Livingstone daisies in his border. They bring a beautiful splash of colour – purple, yellow, red, pink – to the garden.

"They are lovely while they last," Harry explained. "But I wouldn't want to be like them."

I asked why not.

"They put on a fine display when the sun shines," he told me, "but they diminish and close when the weather gets grey.

"Then they come back when the sun shines again. That's OK for flowers, but who needs a friend like that?"

No delicate daisy is my friend Harry.

Wednesday – July 17

WHEN we are ill, it's all too easy to mope and moan. John Donne, the 16th-century poet, would have had every reason to feel miserable and do nothing while suffering from typhus.

Instead, he wrote the "Devotions", including this uplifting passage:

"All of mankind is of one author and one volume; when one man dies, one chapter is not torn out of the book, but translated into a better language; and every chapter must be so translated . . .

"God's hand is in every translation; and His hand shall bind up all our scattered leaves again for that library where every book shall lie open to one another."

Thursday – July 18

SHEILA had been working in a voluntary organisation. The people she worked with were a real mixed bag.

Tom seemed to set out to aggravate her, so she wasn't at all upset when he stopped showing up.

She saw him again three years later.

"I took to heart that thing you said," he told her. "I went to college. I've got myself a job I love. I just wanted to say thanks."

Of course, Sheila congratulated him.

"I have no idea what 'that thing' I said was," Sheila told me later. "I can't recall ever talking to him about further education. But something I said made a big difference."

That is why we ought to err on the side of the positive whenever we speak. We never know when something we say will really speak to someone.

We make an impression. Make sure it's a positive, life-affirming one.

Friday – July 19

TODAY, I saw a man browsing a supermarket aisle.

"Excuse me," I said. "I don't normally compliment people I don't know, but that is spectacular." I pointed to the butterfly tattoo across his throat. "I like that a lot!"

"Thanks, man," he replied. "Cheers!"

And that would be it – a compliment passed on. But there is a thing that happens when you speak to strangers.

In the split second after the "Excuse me", there will be a response, a look, that tells you something about them. It's an instinctive and honest response.

This man's head went down and there was a look in his eyes that said "What now?" – a look that expected trouble.

My compliment on the tattoo would not have been worth mentioning if it wasn't for the feeling I then had that complaints were much more frequent in this man's life than compliments.

I was doubly glad I had spoken. You never know what a kind word means to someone until you actually offer it.

Saturday – July 20

No matter the sea crashes and roars
And the waves whip and lash at the walls,
The lighthouse light keeps turning,
Ignoring the wild sea's calls.
The parallel – are our lives set adrift
As we face the staggering storm?
When will it cease, we cry out,
Till on wings of peace we are borne?
But it was always there, the beacon of light,
Though threat obscures the view –
The love of the Lord will sustain us
As he steers us through
Sweet harbours new.

Dorothy McGregor

Sunday – July 21

THE castle sat atop the hill. Impressive, but ruined. The wildflowers on the hill were new. They would beautify the slopes and feed the bees, who spread those flowers far and wide.

New generations of pollinators would be born. The cycle would repeat and, hopefully, expand each succeeding year.

Castles were once the pinnacle of man's achievement, destined only to crumble. But God's work bears fruit; it goes on, increases.

Hopefully, as a people, we are now learning our real defence comes more from the latter than the former.

Monday – July 22

IT was an overheard conversation in a coffee shop. The first person was stressing the importance of caring for one another.

The second person was more dismissive.

"I've always cared for others, but it seems no-one cares for me. So what's the point?"

"The point is," the first person answered, "which would you rather be, a person who cares or a person who doesn't care?"

Our choices affect us more than anyone else. Choose to care.

Tuesday – July 23

WE are lucky enough, on occasion, to travel across "the pond" to visit our friends Leroy and Sue in Pennsylvania.

On the wall of their kitchen, they have advice from William Penn, the founder of the state. The advice comes from his book "Some Fruits Of Solitude". To paraphrase, it suggests that we:

Think twice before speaking once, and you will speak twice as well.

Rarely promise, but always deliver.

Do good with what you have, or it will do you no good.

Love is the hardest lesson. For that reason we should try hardest to learn it.

Wednesday – July 24

ACCORDING to the legend, the English writer and philosopher G.K. Chesterton was reading his morning newspaper when the editor asked, "What is wrong with the world today?"

Chesterton sent a reply off that same day. It read, "Dear sir. I am."

I don't believe Chesterton – or any one person – can be held responsible for the ills of the world.

I do believe we can each be responsible for how kind we are, how honest we are, and so on. If we each let our personal standards slip, then the standards of the world slip.

But if we each lift them higher . . .

Thursday – July 25

ISOBEL is always busy these days. She was a post-war baby, but she also had four sisters who were born before World War II.

"Which meant," she told me, "that, growing up, it was like I had four extra mothers.

"My sisters practised their child-rearing skills on me. They're not all with us now, and the ones who are need a lot of help.

"Now, I get to do for them what they did for me."

The cared-for has become the carer. We are loved and we return love in due time, all being well.

Friday – July 26

IN his poem "Scaffolding", Seamus Heaney described the care with which builders put scaffolding together.

After all, they need to be safe to work. Once the work is done, the scaffolding is pulled down and taken away.

Many are the "boards" and "poles" we use when building our relationships, and they change with time.

Shared activities might fall out of favour. Different interests come into play. Distance might render the "scaffolding" ineffective.

But if the structure we created while all those things were in place is well built, then our friendships will stand regardless.

Saturday – July 27

I FOUND myself in charge of a three-month-old baby recently. What surprised me most about it was the number of people who spoke to me!

I've noticed this phenomenon before. People who see you and have nothing to tell what sort of character you are might walk past.

If they see you in charge of a little one, they know that someone trusts you and that you will do this much, at least, in love.

It tells me that people want to be sociable, want to talk, and be kind – if they have some clue that it's OK to do so.

A baby might not always be handy, but a smile and a pleasant demeanour might help fill that gap.

Sunday – July 28

I FIRST found this list of "spiritual remedies" over 30 years ago, which is still relevant today.

"Can I have a little more common sense, to take people as they are. Cheerfulness, to share my happiness instead of my sorrows.

"Humility, to do God's work when I would rather be looking to my own comfort. Perseverance, to keep doing the above.

"Prayer, to leave a space in my heart where God can speak and I can listen."

A little more can make a big difference!

Monday – July 29

THE woman in the charity shop queue was buying an LP. The sales assistant looked at the name on the cover and said, "We had a biography of him donated recently. Would you like to see it?"

The woman shook her head.

"I like listening to him sing," she replied. "But the less I know about his personal life, the better."

It takes talent and perseverance to become a world-renowned singer.

It takes so much more to live a life as pure and beautiful as a song.

Most of us won't have people singing our songs after we pass on, but perhaps we will have people singing in praise of the lives we lived.

Tuesday – July 30

IT was a space where play had been actively discouraged. In the little area between the garages and the houses, three trees grew, but the ground around them had been filled with concrete and round stones to make it difficult to walk on.

Some imaginative child had placed a table and a little chair there, creating two flat surfaces. The table bore a little tea set.

Where the ground was nothing pleasant to look at, the child had decorated the low-hanging branches of the trees with ribbons, flags and soft toys.

There is no obstacle to a creative child's imagination!

Wednesday – July 31

KAREN and Eddie were discussing sending love out into a world that sometimes didn't seem to care.

"It will come back to you in some other guise," Karen insisted.

Eddie was obviously unimpressed.

"Still, if all that happens is that you get better at loving . . ." he replied ". . . well, that's not nothing, I suppose."

It's not nothing. It's very much something!

August

I WAS – who knows why – reading diet and exercise advice from the 1930s, when it seemed the world was changing far too rapidly.

The writer talked about the merits of walking as opposed to taking the charabanc, then discussed various dietary changes that had come about.

"Then we have the vegetarians," she wrote, "the fruitarians, the no-breakfast or no-lunch brigade, and others too numerous to mention, but who are all assured they have discovered the elixir of life."

I expected her to be disparaging, but she ended: "It is a happy state to be in, so they must be left alone."

How refreshing, I thought, to find someone living differently and not to try to correct or condemn them, but simply acknowledge it works for them and does no harm.

We might take this "dietary" advice to heart in other aspects of life.

Friday – August 2

ASK the parent of young children and they will tell you that happiness is a good night's sleep, or getting the house tidy.

Ask a lover, and they will tell you happiness is time spent with their beloved.

For some, happiness is found in the little things – a cup of tea, a few minutes with your feet up, a call from a friend.

Of course, it can be the small things and the big things.

Greek philosopher Aristotle summed it up perfectly when he wrote, "Happiness is the meaning and purpose of all life, the whole aim and end of human existence."

There are many who think the purpose of life is something else. If that's you, does the something else make you happy? I'm sure it does!

Happiness can be found in moments of peace and all the little things.

Thursday – August 15

FILM star Charles Bronson grew up in poverty. He joined the Army, then made a name for himself in the movies.

A young Kurt Russell, hearing it was Bronson's birthday, bought him a gift.

Bronson put the package down, looked at it, looked at Russell, then left.

Later, he explained that no-one had ever given him a birthday gift before.

If people don't behave as we expect they ought, allow for the possibility that their experiences in life might have been very different from ours.

Friday – August 16

JAMES WEDGWOOD DRAWBELL was a playwright and a journalist in the mid 1900s.

In his memoir "Drifts My Boat", he describes how Winston Churchill once sent him a note of appreciation from 10, Downing Street.

As impressive as that must have been, Drawbell noted that it would have been written at the same time as Churchill was preparing for the Battle of Britain.

No matter the pressure of "work", we can always find time to be pleasant!

Saturday – August 17

THE couple had lived in the house for a few years before getting new windows and doors.

Once the house was back in order, they talked about how fresh it all looked and how they both planned to take greater care of the property now. The new windows and doors almost demanded it.

It's a very human instinct to care more for the new and the fresh – and what you paid for!

It's slightly better than human instinct – something to aspire to – to care for the familiar, what might be past its prime, and what was once fresh and new for someone else.

How colourless our lives would be
Without the joy of flowers;
Their beauty and their perfume
So enrich this world of ours.

They brighten up our city parks
With colour and with scent,
And make the daily working grind
Seem somehow more well spent!

Flowers comfort us in times of grief
When hearts are filled with pain;
Their fragile beauty makes us hope
That we'll find peace again.

And weddings would not be the same
Without bright blooms galore,
So flowers enrich each part of life –
A joy for ever more.

Eileen Hay

Monday – August 19

AN agony aunt from a popular magazine in the 1930s told of a letter she received from "a prodigal son".

He knew that she sometimes gave talks at various Women's Guilds in her area.

Writing from overseas, he asked her to pass on a message to the mothers at these guilds.

"Never stop praying, because we never get away from it," he wrote. "We try, but we don't succeed.

"When some of my pals gather in my shack in this God-forsaken land, we don't talk about what we are doing, or going to do," he continued, "but only about what we have left and lost."

We might not speak to our "lost sheep", but the bonds of prayer are just as important now as they were then.

Don't you agree?

Trying your best can lead to new, wonderful results!

Tuesday – August 20

THE local politician was talking about building bridges between the divided parts of a community.

It was all very positive stuff, but some people are never happy.

"If you are a bridge," one of the audience members – perhaps cynical, or perhaps with an interest in maintaining separation – shouted, "you will get walked all over by both sides."

"My dear sir," the politician replied with a smile. "That is the point and purpose of bridges. Always has been!"

The heckling came to a halt, and the chances of unity increased.

Wednesday – August 21

I AM paying for two teas and two chocolate muffins, please," I said.

"Did you enjoy them?" the woman behind the till asked me.

"Very much," I replied. "We admired the fine chocolate latticing over the muffins. Very delicate – and tasty, too."

"The baker was off today," she admitted. "Usually the chocolate goes into the muffins, but I didn't know how to do that, so . . ."

Too many people know how things ought to be done, and stick to that.

Sometimes not knowing, but trying the best you can, creates a whole new – often better – way of doing things.

Thursday – August 22

WHY rush to view the Pyramids or climb the Eiffel Tower,
When I can see God's handiwork in meadow, tree and flower?
I'll wait to walk the Inca trail or cruise around the Med:
Finding beauty close to home, I'll rest in my own bed.
Adventures are exciting and I've had some in the past,
The memories of the places I've visited still last.
But, for now, while all I truly love is here with me,
There's nowhere else in this whole world I really need to be.

Laura Tapper

Friday – August 23

JAMES ANTHONY FROUDE was a friend and biographer of the great writer Thomas Carlyle.

When Carlyle's wife, Jane, died, Froude paid a visit.

He sat down next to Carlyle, found himself at a loss for words, but sat there an hour before he left.

The next day, Carlyle sent a note, thanking Froude for his understanding.

Never let not being able to do anything stop you from doing nothing when the time is right.

Saturday – August 24

THE little "Book Of Common Prayer" was worn and well used. The inscription read, "For your birthday, John. With love from Mummy", and it was dated 1940, when the world was at war.

What caught my attention when I found it in the charity shop was that it was covered in old-fashioned brown wrapping paper, held together by sticking tape that had almost ceased to exist.

I wondered – had it been sent to John at the Front?

What better to send to a soul in such troubled times, when there was nothing else that could be done, than a prayer?

Sunday – August 25

ENGLISH poet and minister Richard Watson Dixon wrote "Love's Consolation" around 1869.

In it he says:

"There is one way for thee; but one; inform thyself of it; pursue it . . . Nothing bars a man who goes the way he should go."

In other words, we should find the purpose God has in mind for us, and follow it.

An anonymous annotator added that the "way" for them was the way "home", or to heaven.

If there was one way, laid before you by God, what way would it be?

Monday – August 26

HE held his newborn baby in his arms and she cried.

Perhaps she was cold, perhaps she needed fed, or perhaps she was just in shock at this brand-new world.

But he just beamed with pride and love.

If I could have asked for one wish at that moment, it would be that he remembered that pride and love through all the difficult times in the years ahead.

Because, whatever the problems, she would still be his baby, and he would still be her daddy.

Then I wondered, in that moment, if I had let any of my own loves slip.

Tuesday – August 27

THE organisers of these regular musical events usually ask their audiences to bring along a donation for the food bank.

I collect the resultant – usually generous – offerings from the venue.

This time, however, the entire collection consisted of three tins and one packet, in all likelihood a one-person effort.

It could have been sad, yet it was a reminder that every collection, no matter how large or small, is the result of individual efforts.

As long as one person cares, I shall not give up hope!

Wednesday – August 28

THE castle had been a preserved monument for longer than it was ever an active fortification.

Where once enemies had laid siege and anxious soldiers paced battlements in the night, now smiling families had picnics there, other people walked dogs or craned their necks to take photographs, dozens of children played hide and seek, and flowers grew.

As a once young and reckless man who is now enjoying a lengthy old age, I patted the stone of a gateway without a gate and it seemed to me that we agreed: it's better this way!

Here's to a long and peaceful retirement!

Castle Sinclair Girnigoe in the north of Scotland.

Thursday – August 29

MY goodness! You think you know a thing or two, then you try answering questions set by a two-year-old!

"Why are there birds on this field and not that field?"

"Why is the path green, but only on that side?"

"Why must caterpillars turn into butterflies?"

They won't be satisfied with, "Just because."

It reminds me of how much I simply "assume" I know.

Perhaps I'd be a wiser man if I saw the world as a two-year-old, asked a few more questions, and tried to explain the answers to myself!

Friday – August 30

IT was a beautiful bronze garden ornament, shaped like a boy drinking from a fountain.

It was meant to operate as a fountain, but obviously hadn't for some time.

A spider's web stretched from the boy's nose to the water hole.

Of course, there could be many good reasons why it wasn't being used, but it did make me think as I walked on by.

The ways of life should be kept in continuous flow, or the ways of death will surely take over.

Saturday – August 31

THERE'S a story that says the radio operator on the liner *Queen Elizabeth II* once received a message from the liner the *Queen Mary*. But the message was 40 years old!

Radio experts debate the possibility of a message like that bouncing around the atmosphere for such a long time.

The general conclusion is that it might be possible, or it might not. No-one knows for sure.

I do know that the things we put out into the world have a habit of reaching people we never expected.

As good a reason as any to think twice before we act!

September

WHEN C.S. Lewis wrote "The Lion, The Witch And The Wardrobe", he dedicated it to his goddaughter Lucy.

He admitted that she might be too grown up for fairy stories, but hoped that one day she'd be old enough to start reading them again.

Our middle years tend to be taken up with busyness and with achieving stuff, but our earlier and later years tend to be more philosophical.

Could it just be that, at those ages, we feel closer to the real stuff – the things our middle years try so hard to distract us from?

There's more to life than the world would have us know. I know it and the young ones know it.

Those in the middle? They'll remember some day.

COLIN likes to talk. Jen usually puts up with it. But they were on a tight schedule, to climb and descend the mountain before dark.

Just after they started, Colin stopped to talk to a walker coming down the hill.

An hour later, he stopped to talk to another descending walker. An hour after that he was chatting again.

"We'll never get to the top," Jen complained, "if you stop to talk with everybody we meet."

"I asked the first walker what the weather was like at the top," Colin explained. "He said it was fine. I asked the second walker the same question. She said it was blowy. I asked the third walker. He said it was fierce."

Colin and Jen turned back, making it to the hostel before the storm hit.

Listening to those who walked the path before them kept them safe. For once, Jen was glad that Colin likes to talk.

Tuesday – September 3

I DO like a map, and the older the better.

I enjoy poring over the details, imagining how it must have been, comparing it mentally with how it is.

But a challenge set by French philosopher Gaston Bachelard made me stop and wonder if I was up to it.

"Each one of us," he suggested, "should make a surveyor's map of his lost fields and meadows.

"In this way we cover the universe with drawings we have lived."

Where to begin? Which of your lost meadows would you draw first, and what would you include in it?

Wednesday – September 4

LILLIAN and her mum didn't have the best of relationships. The mother frustrated the daughter in so many ways.

In latter years, Mum lost her sight, so Lillian read her correspondence for her, and read her magazines and books out loud.

"It was a reversal of the bedtime stories she used to read me," Lillian explained. "But it was more.

"As I read the things that interested her, that mattered to her, at first I was just helping, but gradually I began to get it, and see why it all mattered."

Mum's gone to heaven now, but a new closeness and depth of understanding stayed behind in Lillian's heart.

Thursday – September 5

SHE thanked the man profusely, adding, "You really are a godsend!"

He stopped, thought about it for a moment, then replied.

"Oh, I really hope so!"

Imagine living your life like everything you did was done on behalf of a kind and loving God.

Now, do more than just imagine it. Because you can. And it will make a difference.

Friday – September 6

I WAKE up every morning full of hope
That, trusting in your guidance, Lord, I'll cope
With obstacles which block the way ahead,
Or worries that might strike my heart with dread.
For while my faith assures me you are near
My courage always overcomes my fear.
There's joy to be discovered every day
In love and beauty, laughter, work and play,
Till stars come out and I lie down to rest
I give you thanks, for I am truly blessed.

Laura Tapper

Saturday – September 7

HARRY was washing graffiti off the gable end of a friend's house. "How frustrating is that?" I asked.

"About a minute's worth," he replied.

"I've been here for twenty minutes. It took me a minute to consider every aspect of this nonsense.

"The other nineteen have gone into thinking about how this wall was built, and how well it was built."

Destruction takes a bad mood. Construction takes foresight, planning, skill and effort. Which deserves the most attention?

Sunday – September 8

A COUPLE I know were having a baby. Early scans showed problems with the baby's development.

Every scan afterwards showed the same. The problems were numerous and the baby wouldn't live long beyond birth.

An operating room and a five-year plan of further operations were set up.

When the child was born, she was healthy.

Dad asked the doctor for an explanation.

The doctor shrugged and said, "Count your blessings."

"I'll count the prayers that were said for her," Dad replied.

Monday – September 9

AFTER a visit to Abbotsford, the wonderfully preserved and renovated home of Sir Walter Scott, I spent an hour or two perusing a book I bought there.

This publication described the renovation in words and pictures.

I noted the entry on the "Religious Corridor", which had latterly been used for the storage of chairs, coal scuttles, fire-guards "and anything else that needed hidden out of the way".

May our own religious walk be on full display and active, rather than hidden away and forgotten about.

Tuesday – September 10

THE Lady Of The House's Great-aunt Louisa wrote about a "wag at the wa'" in her diary.

She had found the term in a novel where the author was speaking of a pendulum clock.

"He, or rather his character," she wrote, "insisted that their wag at the wa' would work properly for a lifetime, on one or two conditions.

"These were that it should be blown through occasionally with a bellows, and have its working stroked – again, occasionally – with a lightly oiled feather.

"One wonders how the ordinary person would fare," she went on, "left to get on with their work, and being offered only such gentle correction."

Gentleness often exceeds expectations.

Wednesday – September 11

IT'S called "The Apache Wedding Blessing", but it was written by Elliott Arnold in 1947 for his novel "Blood Brother".

The source of the words might matter less than the use we put them to. Imagine if we treated each other like this:

"Now you will feel no rain, for each of you will be a shelter to the other. Now you will feel no cold, for each of you will be warmth to the other."

Thursday – September 12

ON a country ramble with three small walkers, we found a dead bird. The little walkers gathered around and cried for it.

I didn't. Walking on, I wondered why not. After all, a beautiful part of creation had ended.

I told myself I'd had other responsibilities.

I knew I had witnessed worse tragedies, but it occurred to me that those children still had something I seemed to have lost.

That awe, that appreciation, that tenderness – would I be better for rediscovering or recreating it?

I'd like to find out.

Friday – September 13

AT the end of the day, falling into bed is usually a very enticing prospect.

But there is something better than that – if I have the will-power.

To take a few minutes and cast my mind back over the waking hours, remembering the pleasures shared, the work done, and asking, "Did I make the day even a little better?"

If no wonderful achievement springs immediately to mind, then there might be a teacup or two to wash and dry.

It doesn't take much to leave the day a little better than you found it, and you will sleep better for taking the time to think of it.

Saturday – September 14

DO I know any geniuses? It seems like I might, but they aren't scientists or mathematicians or the like.

There's one who works in the pet shop. I have one as a neighbour, and then there is our dear friend, Mary.

What am I talking about? It's a quote I saw recently, attributed to the great writer Aldous Huxley.

It said, "The secret of genius is to carry the spirit of childhood into old age, which means never losing your enthusiasm."

Are you a genius?

Sunday – September 15

IN an essay, J.B. Priestley described a visit to the Royal Albert Hall, where he sat in "the Gods". He observed that the musicians and conductor appeared so small they hardly seemed to be human.

Perhaps, he thought, that was why "so many good Roman citizens could watch unmoved the atrocities of the arena, because the places were so big."

Distance can be good for the bigger picture, but it does separate us from the smaller things – like people. It is sometimes deemed necessary, especially when unpleasant actions have been taken.

If we would deal with our fellow humans more kindly, more fairly, we should come down from the heights of judgement and see them as God sees them, as he knows them. Get closer.

Monday – September 16

APPARENTLY, when the thriller writer John le Carré was asked by a ten-year-old boy how he might become a spy, le Carré suggested he aim higher and avoid the dishonesty inherent in spying.

The same excitement, he suggested, might be found if the boy decided on a great cause and dedicated himself to it.

That way, he would become a good and happy man.

Good advice for a ten-year-old. Good advice no matter what our age!

Tuesday – September 17

HE was talking about truth to his grandson, but the boy couldn't see beyond the short-term gain a lie might bring.

He told a story of a teacher of his who'd said, "I know you to be an honest boy. If you tell me it's the truth, I'll believe you."

Reinforcing a lie his friends had told, he'd replied, "It's the truth."

"My shame at that deceit has outlived many of the friends it was made for," he told his grandson now.

"Nothing short-term about that."

He thinks the point was taken.

The grandeur of large spaces can help us see the bigger picture.

The interior of the Royal Albert Hall.

Wednesday – September 18

WE stood in the street. A man walked up his garden path, watching us all the way.

Reaching his door, he didn't go in. He stood there, staring.

"Uh oh," I muttered. "Nosy neighbour alert. He probably thinks we're 'casing the joint'."

"Excuse me!" my sweetheart shouted. "We're looking for . . ."

His suspicious expression softened.

"I was just about to ask if you needed help," he replied.

I wondered if anyone looking at my relaxed expression ever saw a cynical, suspicious man.

I hope they would be as wrong in their judgement as I was.

Thursday – September 19

IT sounds like a myth, but the person who told it declared it true.

A theatre technician was watching as comedian Billy Connolly entertained his audience. Several times, Billy consulted a sheet of paper at the back of the stage.

Thinking this must be his set list, the technician resolved to take it as a souvenir when the show was over.

When he reached it, though, he found it wasn't a list of sketches, but just these three words – "Say something funny!"

We could do worse than to keep such a set list on the stage of our lives; advice to be consulted whatever situation you find yourself in.

I might recommend three different words: "Say something kind".

Friday – September 20

THE Zoom meeting opened with a prayer. The person praying talked about the call to come to Jesus as little children and about the wonder of seeing the world as a child might.

On one of the screens, a woman raised her hand, requesting to be unmuted. She lifted her grandchild, who'd been asleep on her lap.

Faces brightened and hardened attitudes melted. Somehow, the meeting was smoother, happier and more cooperative than expected.

Saturday – September 21

THE foundations of the folly can still be found in the hilltop grass. The family who once owned the land had designed the columned viewpoint, then planted trees on every side of the conical hill.

Grassy alleyways between the planted areas allowed views of their favourite parts of the estate.

Turn this way and you saw their dovecot, this way their purpose-built lake, this way the stables.

The trees themselves blocked any view of the laundry, the mine works and the homes of tenant farmers.

Imagine you were the folly at the top of the hill of your life. What would you be looking at? What would you be hiding?

As you grew older, would you be planting more trees or opening up more views?

Sunday – September 22

THE play "The Way Of The World" by William Congreve is what a modern audience might call a "rom-com", but it made its stage debut in 1700.

Reading through it, I noticed the casual use, by a servant to her husband, of the phrase "B'w'y".

What did it mean? It's a shortened version of "God be with you".

More than three centuries later, we still shorten the same phrase. We pronounce it "goodbye".

In other words, when I can't be there to care for you, may God be with you. He will be!

Monday – September 23

IT was a film rather than real life, but the older woman had wronged the younger one.

The younger one got revenge by becoming just like the older one. Then she declared, "I'm not like her. I'm better!"

Beating our enemies at their own game isn't being better. Try "beating" them at a kinder game. Not easy, but it is better!

WOULD you like a bunch of roses?"
The handsome young man then went on to spoil the romance a little.

"They are about to go past their sell-by date, and my manager says I've got to get rid of them."

So Julie took the roses home from the supermarket.

She put them in a jug of water, but the next two days were busy and she forgot about them.

They looked quite sorry for themselves when she eventually got around to tending to them.

But with some plant food, judicious snipping and a pretty vase, they actually looked quite lovely.

"I just applied some TLC," she told me.

"And what a difference it has made," I replied.

"I don't believe in sell-by dates," she explained. "Especially when it comes to people.

"Too often I have seen people think they are at the end of their 'shelf-life', only to bloom again thanks to some tender loving care."

BACK in the 1930s, the popular romance writer Annie S. Swan wrote:

"In the heart of almost every woman, there is a house of remembrance, one which she holds especially dear.

"Perhaps it is only a cottage on a hillside or in some country lane . . .

"It may even be only a room in a tenement, to which she came as a young wife and where little children have been born.

"But it is a home she never forgets and to which her heart never grows cold."

I would venture it isn't only women who have such a "house of remembrance".

Warm remembrance, if we have been fortunate.

Where might yours be?

Tending for flowers, and others, can help them bloom!

Thursday – September 26

IN Neil Munro's novel "The Daft Days", set in the 1800s, the Dyce family prepare to welcome an orphaned relative to Scotland.

The child's two aunties wonder how best to school them.

Should they teach "God Save The Queen", encourage speaking with a "proper" Scottish accent and send them to university so they might become a lawyer?

The child's uncle insists there is a more important thing to be learned.

"The first thing to do with your nephew," Daniel Dyce insists, "is to teach him to be happy, for it's a habit that has to be acquired early."

I learned that habit early myself. And I like to think I have shared the lesson often.

Friday – September 27

I HAVE been told I am too liberal with compliments. Myself, I see it as an enthusiasm for what is good.

In one of those studies that leaves us wondering who undertook them and why, it was decided that it takes 21 compliments to recover the good feeling stripped away by one criticism.

I might question the validity of the study, but the conclusion seems about right.

We live in an extremely critical world. Those of us inclined to compliment have our work cut out for us.

Saturday – September 28

JAMES BOSWELL, the 18th-century Scottish lawyer, is quoted as saying, "We must take our friends as they are."

No doubt it's a kind thing to do, and we would feel quite virtuous turning a blind eye to the many and varied shortcomings of those who would be our friends.

It's a rather more humbling – but nonetheless, lovely – thought that perhaps they do the same for us.

Do as you would be done by. For friendship's sake.

Sunday – September 29

THE girl was eight years old and had been elected on to her year's school council. She regularly got stars for her good work.

But her parents didn't like it.

"Where's the humility in any of that?" they asked me earnestly. "This new attitude of self-worth – we don't agree with it."

So every time she won a prize, her parents reminded her that lots of people were doing better, in an effort to stop her getting conceited.

I know where they are coming from, and I also know better than to argue with that attitude.

How about this for an alternative? We are wonderfully made by a wonderful God; the glory of God is surely a life lived to the full.

That wee girl is a wonderful creation.

The humility comes into it when we realise that everyone else is as well, and that all we are is a gift!

You can humbly believe that you are no better than anyone else and still have that be an amazing thing!

Monday – September 30

I LOVE it inside churches,
Absorbing that singular smell;
The quiet, calming atmosphere
Assures me all is well.
The vibrant, fragrant flowers,
Plaques to people gone before,
I wonder about the lives they led –
Were they rich or poor?
The gentle playing of the organ,
Click of heel on ancient tile;
The cheerful chiming of the bells
Is sure to make me smile.
I love it inside churches,
The pews polished, glowing warm.
Churches are my comfort,
A true port in any storm.

Susan Blackburn

October

Tuesday – October 1

WORK is very often a means to an end, but sometimes . . . Sarah took a chance and opened a book shop.

When the Lady Of The House and I visited one brisk morning, she was offering a hot chocolate to a girl seated in the children's section.

"Do you have mini marshmallows?" the girl asked.

"She's my granddaughter," Sarah explained to me. "She loves coming to the shop."

I thought of the large proportion of us who work to pay the bills.

But to have a job your grandchildren can come to and be pampered – that's winning the lottery! Providing it makes enough money to keep them going in mini marshmallows!

Wednesday – October 2

I HAVE a very special book –
It's one I'd like to share.
We turn the pages carefully,
The whole of life is there.
Some pages coloured pink and gold,
When youth had hopes and dreams,
And then a touch of grey and black,
With disappointed schemes.
But then the autumn colours glow
With warmth and hope and joy,
And love shines out from every page –
A love we can't destroy.
But there are empty pages left,
What stories will they tell?
They must be handled carefully
And we must treat them well.

Iris Hesselden

Thursday – October 3

THE baby had one of those multi-textured cloth toys. At first I thought it was a caterpillar, then I saw the markings. It was an inchworm.

In the 1952 film "Hans Christian Andersen", Danny Kaye sings to an inchworm busy "measuring the marigold".

With a backing of schoolchildren learning to count, he tells the little creature that, with its superior arithmetic skills, it's bound to go far, but that it might stop occasionally to see how beautiful the marigolds actually are.

If I sang the baby the song a few times, it was just to help him get an early start on a life of appreciation.

Friday – October 4

CHINESE tradition supposedly has it that we live our lives in twelve-year segments.

After our first five "ages" – in other words, by the time we are sixty – we are reckoned to be physically and materially complete.

Our responsibilities are old enough to take care of themselves, and we can devote ourselves to a little "soul gardening", cultivating our spiritual wellbeing.

Isn't that a beautiful, uplifting way to look at the senior years?

Saturday – October 5

I WASN'T sure if I'd been insulted or not.

He found me sitting on the low branch of a tree, gazing into the trees as a gentle drizzle fell.

"A nemophilist, I see," he said.

He, at least, had the excuse of a dog to walk, and we exchanged a few words about her before he went on his way.

Arriving home, I looked up his "insult". It's an archaic word, meaning a lover – or a "haunter" – of the woods.

I suppose it was true enough. And why not? After all, the woods haunt me, too, in the most peaceful, soothing way imaginable.

Sunday – October 6

I SPENT some time talking to a shepherd of a bygone generation. He told me about spending the nights on the hill with a sick sheep.

"I'd sit down beside her," he said, "pull me collar up, and pull me hat down. I'd talk to her for a while, then I'd shut up and let the Lord do the talking."

We hadn't mentioned faith up to that point.

He was a tough, no-nonsense fellow, no longer with us, but he knew a thing or two.

Monday – October 7

ENOUGH was enough. I was about to have it out with the fellow and it wouldn't be pretty.

Then I glanced at the calendar and realised it was his birthday.

I couldn't spoil his special day, so I'd wait.

Then that annoying little voice in my head asked, "Is it OK to spoil the day after his special day? Or the day after that?"

Sighing, I bought a card and delivered a gift.

He asked if I wanted to go for a coffee. We chatted, sorted a lot out, and parted as friends.

It's worth remembering that even our "enemies" want to be loved on their birthdays – and every other day.

Tuesday – October 8

THE Lady Of The House saw them in the clothes shop – two young women, one trying on dresses, the other suggesting styles that might suit.

Wonderful, innocent fun. But I knew a little more.

One of the women had just been diagnosed with a tumour a week short of her thirtieth birthday party.

I also knew she had no money and her friend would pay for the dress to lift her spirits.

We paused for a moment and gave thanks, yet again, for the never-ending wonder that is friendship.

Wednesday – October 9

JIMMY finds the ram horns and deer antlers on his walks. He carries a hand-saw in his pocket and chooses the branches with care.

He works the wood and horn with patience and focus in his garage workshop. He even makes the metal ferrules for the tips.

Every couple of months he has a new, elegant, horn-handled walking stick.

Jimmy doesn't need a walking stick, so he cuts it to the required length for the person he has in mind, and he gives it away.

It's only a hobby to Jimmy.

To me, it's a way of making help an art form.

Thursday – October 10

PEOPLE who have had very long hair and then get it cut short tell me there is an unexpected lightness that comes with the experience.

All that hair had a weight they weren't aware of while they were carrying it, but they felt lighter when it was gone.

I wonder if that's what it is like when we let go of a hurt we have carried for a long time.

Friday – October 11

THE internet – that wonderful font of the ridiculous – informs me there is a man who walks around Melbourne city centre hugging a giant carrot.

He has tried carrying other (fake) giant vegetables, but he prefers the carrot.

Why? Simply this. Because it makes people smile and he thinks the world could do with more smiles.

I was tempted to dismiss the story as foolishness.

Then I wondered how many smiles I had brought to the world today.

A giant carrot would certainly have increased the number!

Saturday – October 12

YOU'RE a wise man," I told him. "Your grandchildren will be blessed to have your influence in their lives."

He smiled until I didn't think his cheeks could take the strain any more.

"Ah," he replied at last. "If only it worked that way.

"If my grandchildren have a wise grandfather, it's only because they taught him so much about life while they were discovering it for themselves! Still, I'll do my best."

Sunday – October 13

THERE is an interesting phenomenon that occurs in the middle of the ocean.

When you are as far from land as possible, if you look around, you will see the horizon seems to rise in every direction.

It is as if you sit at the focal point of a lens and it seems that the world is looking at you.

That's how it is with God, whether you are mid-ocean or in the kitchen, whether you are in a crowd or alone on a hilltop.

God's full attention is on you, wanting the best for you.

Been there, done that! Been weirded out by it!

Monday – October 14

THIS is a day when plant pots roll around,
Garden chairs tip over, sprawling on the ground.
This is a day when leaves fly from the trees,
Toss and twirl like dancers, caught up in the breeze.
This is a day to hear the wild waves roar,
To see them swell and break, crashing on the shore.
This is a day for running in the park,
Flying kites with children, home before it's dark.
This is a day to blow away our cares,
Time to pick up plant pots – and the garden chairs.

Jo Stone

All generations can learn from each other.

Tuesday – October 15

WE met at the bus stop. I can only assume he wasn't having a good day.

"I dislike October," he said. "It's a wet and mucky month."

I was too taken aback to agree. I love this time of year.

But I stick with the advice I was offered as a boy.

"If you don't learn to find pleasure in the rain, you will have a lot less pleasure – and the same amount of rain!"

Wednesday – October 16

WHAT if," our dear friend Mary asked as we waited for a bus, "our essential nature is love, and everything else is either a distraction from it, or the struggle to get back to it?"

I looked round at the puddles, the traffic, the shops, and wondered where that came from.

I often wonder what goes on in that head of hers, but when she gives us an insight into it, she leaves plenty going on in this head of mine.

What if we are love?

Thursday – October 17

I ENJOY tales of epic journeys of exploration, particularly on the high seas. I have been struck by references to a class of crew, particularly on old Royal Navy ships, called Idlers.

These were the people not on active duty and not involved in the day-to-day sailing of the ship. They might be artists, writers or scientists, but they might also be cooks and doctors.

The Idlers would often be co-opted into other duties as the need arose and were seen as useful in that way.

But how long would any crew have lasted without their cooks and doctors? Hardly unnecessary roles.

It encouraged me to look for the Idlers in my life – people not directly involved in my day-to-day progress, but without whom the journey might not succeed and, anyway, would hardly be worth making.

Friday – October 18

THE world is an awful place. People aren't to be trusted. There is no respect any more. Surely it will all end soon.

I'm paraphrasing an Assyrian inscription from 2800 years BC. The world didn't end back then, nor is it likely to any time soon.

There were people looking for the worst all that time ago, and there would have been people looking for the best, just as there are now. That's how people are.

The world goes on. The question is, how do we prefer to experience it?

Look for the best, and you will find it!

Saturday – October 19

LOVE words, so I was excited when I heard there were such things as "ghost words". Surely there was a fascinating story behind such a dramatic term.

But no. Ghost words are words in dictionaries that never actually meant what the dictionary says they mean.

Sometimes they are simple spelling mistakes.

What an anti-climax! But it did start me wondering about words we use which might die out from lack of use.

Imagine if "love", or "kindness", or "understanding", or "tolerance" were to become ghosts.

I will do my best to keep them alive. Will you join me?

Sunday – October 20

WOULDN'T have done that, if she hadn't . . ."
"I'd have done better if he hadn't been so . . ."

We could all live like saints if it weren't for other people! But how much is our holiness worth if it fails every time someone annoys us?

Someone once told me, "Other people don't get in the way of your spiritual practice. They *are* your spiritual practice."

You will be tested. If you can pass the tests with love and grace, you will be on the right path.

Monday – October 21

IN his 1952 short story "A Sound Of Thunder", Ray Bradbury has a "time tourist" travel back to when the T-Rex walked the world.

The tourist falls and kills a butterfly, accidentally starting a chain reaction that changes his own time in the year 2055.

A little thing that, given enough time, has a big impact.

It's an idea believable enough (in that fantastical world) that it has appeared in almost every time-travel story since then.

But does it hold true in reality?

Let's try, shall we? We are all time travellers in the same forward direction. So if we make a difference today – in a good way – we can watch how it ripples out across the days, weeks and months.

We can change the future. Change it for the better.

Tuesday – October 22

IT'S a proverb from a previous time – "You should know a man seven years before you stir his fire".

Apparently, it's a warning against over-familiarity. You would be treating the other person's fire, and their poker, like your own.

When I read it, a different thought occurred.

If two people have been friends for a long time, inevitably one will serve, or help, the other in some way. The help or service might be returned in some different fashion.

It's a charming aspect of any long friendship that we each help keep the other's fire burning brightly.

Wednesday – October 23

THE brightly coloured letters are about four feet tall and painted on the gable end of a building that once manufactured explosives. The letters are "K", then "ND".

The urban artist who painted them forestalled my question, explaining, "The space allows any one of us to stand there, and be the "I" in "KIND".

Judging by the queue of young people waiting to be photographed in the gap, I think he might be on to something.

Thursday – October 24

J.B. PRIESTLEY talked of a short story writer who lived in a cottage in the woods "where many a tramp has found a night's lodging and paid for it with a strange tale".

I am an avid reader of short stories and longer ones, but I read less the more I talk to people.

It is no loss. I still get my full quota of stories.

The best are to be found waiting at the bus stop, or at the next table in a tea room, or in an accidental meeting.

Read! By all means, read. But also talk!

Friday – October 25

I WAS in the hospital café, waiting for a friend, feeling as trepidatious as the others seemed.

She came in for a quick cuppa. She was wearing a brightly coloured, dinosaur-patterned dress. Her canvas shoes were a riot of smiley faces.

She finished up and left, leaving us smiling and raising our eyebrows. I hoped she worked on a children's ward.

Some people are natural rays of sunshine. Others, bless them, work very hard at it!

Saturday – October 26

THE organiser of the local playgroup changed job and couldn't keep the group going.

She posted about it on social media, giving a few months' notice to all the parents. Despite the fact the job was a good move for her, she couldn't help feeling she was letting people down.

The replies, which she had expected to be full of disappointment, were full of appreciation.

They talked of friends that had been made, help that had been given, and even lives that had been changed!

Sometimes we focus too much on what we can't do, or what we intend to do next, and forget that the good we have already done is still out there, growing like a flower!

Sunday – October 27

I **SAID** a prayer alongside a boy who spoke with a different accent. At the end of it, he asked me, confused, "Why did you say it like that?"

I finally figured out that I had said "Ah-men", while he and his family only ever said "A-men".

After a little thought, he said, "But that works, too!"

A moment of confusion, a moment of the unfamiliar, but the realisation that both worked.

If only we could extend the same grace and courtesy to those whose worship habits are more different from ours, but nonetheless sincere.

Monday – October 28

T **HE** child was at that age where everything was a question. "It's why, why, why, all day long," his mother complained.

"He's at that age where he can speak well enough to ask," the grandmother explained. "And he understands enough to know that he has everything to learn."

Overhearing this, it dawned on me that I don't know everything yet, so why have I stopped asking why? Perhaps because it annoyed people?

Mother and child might have more fun if they asked questions together. Until, of course, one of them has all the answers.

Tuesday – October 29

I **WAS** up to my elbows in a sink full of suds and thinking myself a lucky man!

In the next room, the Lady Of The House was changing a four-month-old visitor.

She was talking a language I couldn't understand or replicate, but the baby understood and was laughing heartily in response.

That's all it took to remind me of how lucky I was.

In a world of troubles, we should appreciate moments of simple joy whenever we see – or hear – them.

Wednesday – October 30

VISITED the coast with a three-year-old. It was raining and cold – very bleak!

He was entertained by the fact that the wall along the promenade had holes at the bottom so waves that topped the wall had a way back to the sea.

We decided the cormorant on the rock was looking for fish, but the swan probably preferred seaweed.

He told me the ducks that were there could fly, but penguins couldn't, and that humans didn't live in the sea, only fish.

Turning away, he watched a seagull ride the wind over a nearby building.

"Wouldn't it be wonderful to fly?" I asked him.

"Even little birds can fly high, high, high!" he replied.

I could have talked about the differences that enable some birds to soar the high mountains while others stay closer to the ground.

But I remembered that he was a "little bird" himself, so I said, "Yes! Yes, they can."

I hope that, in doing so, I added another feather to his developing wings.

Thursday – October 31

YOU might have heard of sticky willies, the weed that children delight in sticking to each other's clothes.

Another name for them is cleavers, but cleave is just another word for something that sticks to something else.

We "cleave" to one another in difficult times.

Unless you study such things, I imagine that is all you know of the sticky willy – that it sticks!

It was once harvested for medicinal purposes, geese love eating it, its root produces a red dye, its roasted seeds can be used as a coffee substitute and the dried plant used to be a favoured mattress filling, but most of us know only one thing about it.

We sometimes judge people like that, by one thing we know about them, for better or worse.

If that's a foolish idea when it comes to a weed . . .

November

I HAVE a question on All Saints' Day. Are you a saint?
In the church, sainthood is generally awarded after the person's death and, beatified in the process, they are often seen as more than they might have been in life.

But when the Apostle John addressed the saints in the church, he meant living people who had dedicated themselves to the faith.

They were flawed individuals, doing their best for God and the good.

So I ask again: are you a saint?

THE coping stones on the old wall were vaguely triangular and hollow.

When a car bumped the wall, it separated two of the stones, leaving a gap between them. The owner fully intended to repair the damage, but months passed.

When he finally got around to it, he ended up putting his cement and trowel away without using them. Birds had built a nest in the shelter, turning it into a cosy home for the winter.

Damage that can be put to a new and good use is surely no damage at all.

TWO men of different faiths were walking by the sea. The first man declared that his church was *the* church.

"Take a bucket to the shoreline there," the second man replied. "Fill it with salt water, then tell me it is the ocean."

God is more than any of our churches. If he wasn't, if he only belonged to one group, he would hardly qualify for the title.

God can be found everywhere we look.

St Leonard's Church in Charlecote, Warwickshire.

Monday – November 4

DUNCAN believed that modern children don't appreciate how lucky they are. Yet the other day he picked up a notepad, and on the first page was a list of his daughter Gemma's "blessings".

The ten-year-old had all the basics there, like "food", "shelter" and "warm clothes".

"Toys", he was amazed to see, only came in at number seven. "Music", "all living creatures" and "baths" were also included.

But it was blessings 19 and 20 that really brought a lump to his throat.

His "unappreciative" daughter had rounded off her list with "nice parents" and "being loved".

Tuesday – November 5

THE bus driver wasn't having a good day. He'd been quite grumpy when I got on.

Approaching my stop, an elderly lady got up first. She slipped a boiled sweet on to the fares tray, saying, "That's for you, driver."

I watched as his expression went from cynical disbelief to a smile.

Catching up with her in the street, I told her I was impressed by her kindness.

"It was just a little thing," she said before walking on.

True enough, I thought, but with enough little things like that, what a world we could make!

Wednesday – November 6

LOOKING out, he saw it was raining heavily.

He remembered he'd left the garage door open, and there was stuff in there he didn't want to get wet, so he went through the connecting door only to see his five-year-old son sitting there on a Mickey Mouse chair, watching the rain bounce off the driveway.

What did he do? Tell him to get inside? Pull the garage door closed?

No, he brought over a camp chair and sat beside his boy. The smile he got in return will live in his heart for a long time.

Thursday – November 7

FIONA makes beautiful empire biscuits, and it might have been a little insensitive of Robert to mention that she brought them to every gathering they had.

"I found something I am good at," she said. "It's my special thing. What's your special thing, Robert?"

Robert confessed that he could do lots of things, but he didn't have one special thing.

Then he took an empire biscuit and declared how delicious it was.

Being a jack of all trades is a fine thing, but how much more fun would the world be if we each took time to acquire that one special thing worth sharing with others?

Friday – November 8

IN "The Shoes Of Fortune", a novel by the author of the Para Handy stories, Neil Munro, one of the main characters is mortally wounded in a fight.

To his credit, he had been fighting to protect a child.

He is carried to his home, where his last words of advice are: "Be good, be simple, be kind . . . Fifty years to learn it, and I might have found it in my mother's lap."

The most profound lessons are the simplest ones. Our first and often our best classroom is our mothers' laps.

Saturday – November 9

IN the Mark Twain story "Which Was The Dream?", little Bessie asked her mamma what qualifies as a little thing.

"Nothing that grieves us can be called little," her mother replies. "By the eternal laws of proportion a child's loss of a doll and a king's loss of a crown are events of the same size."

This is something to remember when we see others "making a fuss over nothing".

Perhaps it isn't nothing to them. And how lucky are we that we can afford to think of it as such?

Sunday – November 10

I HAVE a high-backed wooden chair in my possession. Before it came to me it belonged to a minister. I loved the idea that so many sermons had been crafted in it.

Similarly, I was impressed to hear about the Friends Of Friendless Churches, who operate in England and Wales. These wonderful souls find the money and skills to preserve many abandoned churches.

They may be abandoned, but think of the vows exchanged there, babies baptised there, prayers of love and despair said there.

Don't tell me those don't imprint on a place. And don't tell me that isn't worth preserving.

Monday – November 11

THE tune "Flowers Of The Forest" is often played at Remembrance Day services. It's an ancient tune, usually played on the bagpipes. The earliest preserved lyrics were written by Jean Elliot in 1756.

One line reads, "The Floo'ers o' the Forest are a' wede (weeded) awa'". The "flowers" that have gone are the men of the land.

Remembering them, she also remembers the women and children who will never enjoy those flowers.

Remember our heroes, and never forget those who love, or loved, our heroes.

Tuesday – November 12

DAD was walking a country lane with his three boys in front of him. Seeing a dog walker approaching, he said, "Single file, boys!"

And nothing happened. They kept walking as they had before and the dog walker made his way between them.

"Single file means one person wide," Dad said when he caught up.

"I was walking single file," his first son said.

"Me, too," said the second and then the third.

Single file times three! Individualism.

Teamwork involves a coming together, a changing of our personal directions, even if only a little, for the greater good.

Wednesday – November 13

WHEN Samuel Johnson compiled his "A Dictionary Of The English Language" (published in 1755), many of the definitions were his own.

We might disagree with the meanings of some words, but I do like his assertion that a "novel" is "a small tale, generally of love".

When we are writing our "story", let's make it one that, should it be read or remembered in the future, would seem like it was "generally of love".

Thursday – November 14

THE book was an old one. The edges of the pages looked like they had been torn rather than cut.

The font was a little on the large side, as was the space between the lines. There were only, on average, seven words per line and twenty lines per page.

Bringing it to the attention of the Lady Of The House, I wondered about the limitations of the printing processes in those days.

"Did it occur to you," she asked, "that this book would have been read by lamp or candlelight? All that white space would have made reading easier."

The light dawned. We like to imagine we know how the other person sees the world, but the reality is often an eye-opener.

Friday – November 15

*L*ET'S *not waste a single minute –*
Life has got such wonder in it.
Lift your eyes and you will see,
God is saying, "This is me."
He's in the golden autumn trees,
He's in the clouds and roaring seas,
He's there when dark night turns to day,
He's there to help us on our way,
He's in the smile of those who care.
Just look around – he's everywhere.

Linda Brown

Saturday – November 16

THE party was almost over and the "auld yins" were waxing philosophical about their most memorable moments.

Someone said, "Climbing Kilimanjaro."

Someone else said, "Getting married in the Dominican Republic."

Others chose their children's births.

"The moment I realised that you take nothing with you from this life, but you leave an awful lot behind," Kevin said. "So I decided to leave as much good stuff as possible."

That's a memorable moment that could change lots of lives – and only for the better.

Sunday – November 17

CONVALESCING at home, the poet and war hero Siegfried Sassoon sat by his parents' fireplace watching his dog sleep.

Moonlight shone through the curtains. The wind sighed across the chimney pot.

He said goodbye to some favourite books, bracing himself for a return to "unmitigated hell".

If our young folk must defend their homes at the cost of never returning to them, if some of them do not have homes worth missing, then those who think they rule have failed in the most awful way.

To honour those who never came home, create a world where no others need to leave.

Monday – November 18

THE old stone bridge is only one lane wide. Cars crossing it must take turns or risk meeting in the middle.

If you look over the side, you will see that the three bases on which its arches rest are easily wide enough for two lanes, but they taper upwards to the part of the bridge we see most of.

Leaning over that wall, it occurred to me how much work is often done behind the scenes for a single, visible act of kindness, or one small good thing.

Tuesday – November 19

JULIE is a young and modern gran, but she recently found herself bathing her six-month-old grandson in the kitchen sink.

Chatting about it later on social media, she mentioned she had been bathed the same way when she was a baby.

"Which of us hasn't had a bath in their gran's kitchen sink?" she asked, adding some laughing emojis.

Among the flood of happy memories that came in reply were a couple of comments simply saying, "I didn't have a gran."

"Very few blessings," she told me, "are so universal that everyone gets to share in them. Which is why we should appreciate the ones we have."

Wednesday – November 20

THE rather well-to-do woman came into the dog sanctuary looking for a replacement for a well-loved pet. She seemed to like one particularly scraggy mongrel.

The staff explained the dog had been in a bad way when it arrived, and also that they would need to do checks to make sure the animal was going to a good home.

"Oh, it's not for me," the woman explained. "It's for the couple who took me in twenty years ago when I was a stray and in a bad way."

The checks will still be made, but with a reference like that . . .

Thursday – November 21

AMY has more than enough stories to remember her dad by. They would often walk together, her asking for tales from his childhood and a world gone by.

"Time and again," she told me, "I asked him to write them down for me. He would laugh and say he was too busy.

"I asked once what was keeping him so busy. He replied, 'Making today's memories.'

"Appreciating the past, but delighting in the present. It will be my abiding memory of him."

Friday– November 22

IT'S a striking description. In the biography "Margaret Ogilvy", J.M. Barrie describes his mother's eyes.

"For when you looked into my mother's eyes you knew, as if He had told you, why God sent her into the world – it was to open the minds of all who looked to beautiful thoughts."

Have you ever seen, and been encouraged by, such eyes?

Or do you, perhaps, look out at the world through similar eyes?

We should do our best to make sure that Margaret Ogilvy's eyes were not the last of that kind.

Saturday – November 23

THERE'S a joke doing the rounds where a child asks his mother if it's the right time to throw his "emergency confetti".

She asks him why he has confetti in his pocket.

"I carry it everywhere," he replies. "You never know when you'll get a chance to celebrate!"

Obviously it is funnier told as a joke, but for me it begged a question. As I go through my days, am I more ready to frown, to look for the potential problem, to give grudging credit, or to celebrate?

I know which I think I am, but do others see me the same way?

If they don't, I'll work on it. If they do, I'll throw some confetti!

Sunday – November 24

THE land had been zoned for building and lorry loads of dirt had been dumped there in preparation.

In the months since, grass and scrub had taken root.

This morning, when I went to walk the dog there, I saw a family of deer grazing. I watched and considered the roads on every side.

I could have walked on, and the deer would have scattered.

Instead, I said a silent prayer, apologising for our treatment of the world, being thankful that it contains such wonders, then I turned, leaving the deer in peace, and walked elsewhere.

It was my morning worship.

Always be ready to celebrate the good in life!

Monday – November 25

WHEN life gets in a muddle and things don't quite go to plan,
We need someone to turn to that we're sure will understand.
If we're brimming with excitement at our latest piece of news,
Or we're faced with a decision, full of doubt which path to choose,
It's wonderful to know we always have a trusted friend
With sound advice, a cheery smile, a listening ear to lend.
It's great that we can share our lows and celebrations, too
So as the years go by, we stick together – me and you.

Laura Tapper

Tuesday – November 26

IN his poem "Cargoes", John Masefield writes about sunlit Mediterranean ships loaded with "ivory, and apes and peacocks", emeralds, diamonds and gold.

Then he tells of a British coaster "butting through the Channel in the mad March days" carrying coal, "firewood, iron-ware and cheap tin trays."

Masefield makes no comment. One, undoubtedly, sounds the more exotic, but which would be the most use to the most people?

As we sail through this life, in whatever state, we might consider our cargo.

Wednesday – November 27

I WAS talking to an acquaintance of mine when she smiled and took me by surprise.

It's a thing she rarely does. Her natural inclination, it seems, is to be dour and cynical, as if always expecting the worst. Other folk I know seem predisposed to smile first and be suspicious later.

The first kind of person usually thinks the second quite foolish. Why be so happy when things are bound to go wrong, someone is bound to swindle you, or the sky will fall in at any moment?

The famous author H.G. Wells considered it thus: when things are going badly, anyone with any sense ought to be happy. Things might get better, but even if the whole world comes crashing down around you and you're left with nothing, at least you will have been happy!

Thursday – November 28

IN a box of second-hand novels, I found a personal diary with drawings of pirates and footballers on the cover. It was tatty, as it was entitled to be. It was dated 1937.

The day-to-day thoughts of a boy living in the run-up to World War II, and living a lifestyle long gone, would surely have been fascinating to read, but I wasn't inclined to pry.

I already knew as much about the young fellow as I needed to.

Inside the front cover he had written in a neat hand, "Let me make this day worthwhile for someone else."

I didn't need to read his diary to know he lived a good life. In that simple thought he was already halfway there.

Friday – November 29

THE church steeple caught my eye. It had some sort of cage round the top, and there was a man in it!

On closer inspection the cage was scaffolding, skilfully fitted to the top of the spire where stonemasons were carrying out renovations.

My inquiries won an invitation to climb the steeple and see my home town as I never had before.

I told my friends and family about it, but each looked confused. What cage? What scaffolding? They'd been so busy with day to day stuff that they hadn't noticed what was going on above them.

Oh, what we miss when we don't take the time to look up.

Saturday – November 30

THE family of eight slept in one bed and each had their specific spot. For this little girl, it was the bottom right-hand corner.

A charity built them a new home with beds for each of them. Some time afterwards, my friend visited to see how they were getting on.

The little girl was asleep in the bottom right-hand corner of her own bed. It was where she felt she belonged.

When I see someone who lives their life other than the rest of us, I remember her and tell myself I have no idea what shaped them that way, and I should just be kind.

Focus on building bridges for the future – whether they be physical or spiritual.

Knaresborough Viaduct, Yorkshire.

Shutterstock.

December

Sunday – December 1

THREE-YEAR-OLD Kaden goes on a lot of car journeys with his grandparents.

They could play videos to entertain him in the back of the car, but he prefers to look out for trucks, diggers and especially bridges.

He likes to guess which ones are "people bridges", which are for cars, and so on. A railway bridge is a rare treat.

He even speculated that one might possibly be a "boat bridge", and now they cannot wait to show him an aqueduct with barges on.

Seeing his real interest, his grandad, who is a retired engineer, started talking about the structure, purpose and foundations of bridges.

His grandma, who is a vicar, did the same with the idea of bridges between people, and between people and God.

"It will be interesting to see which he grows up working on," she told me. "After all, they both need to be built."

Monday – December 2

AT this time of year, there is magic in the air.
It would be a closed heart, or a poor unfortunate soul, who didn't acknowledge it.

I won't list the opportunities for experiencing that magic; I'll let you discover them for yourself. But I will agree with Louis L'Amour, who wrote in his mediaeval drama "The Walking Drum" that "this was what made life: a moment of quiet, the water falling in the fountain, the girl's voice . . . a moment of captured beauty. He who is truly wise will never permit such moments to escape."

I can only add that he or she who is truly appreciative will take such moments and use them to heal the hearts of those who never see them.

Tuesday – December 3

IT was a morning when I would rather have stayed at home, but dogs must be walked and will accept no excuses.

I wrapped up: woolly hat, gloves, stout walking boots. Then we ventured out.

I try to find joy in as many things as I can, but this day was bleak. While my four-legged walking partner explored a world of scents, I looked around at low, grey clouds and bare branches.

Deciding to plough on, I tripped. Grass that had grown long in the summer and been knocked flat by wintry winds had tangled the toe of my boot.

I looked down and there was the joy of a bleak winter's day. Beneath the colourless long, washed-out blades – and protected by them – were fresh, green shoots, already preparing for the next season.

You could say it put a spring in my step!

Wednesday – December 4

HE'S a considerate man, but he drove across over a pedestrian crossing when someone was on it.

To make matters worse, the other man was walking with a crutch.

Both were heading to the supermarket and, embarrassed, he considered driving on. Instead, he met the other man at the front door, introducing himself as "the one who almost ran you down".

The other man said, "Oh, yes. I swore at you."

He apologised again, making no excuses. Then they talked about the other man's knee operation and how it wasn't healing well.

"I have two cars I can't drive now," the other man told him. "And I suppose I'm not always perfect when I do drive."

They met again at the checkout and he offered the other man a lift. The other man said he only lived across the road, but that it was nice to have met him.

"We all make mistakes," my friend said. "Sometimes we hide from them and leave them as scars on the day.

"Sometimes we try to heal those wounds. Sometimes it works."

We never know until we try.

Thursday – December 5

I'M not much into wars and battles, but "frontiersman poet" Joaquin Miller caught my attention with his poem "The Greatest Battle That Ever Was Fought".

It needed no army, and was led by no generals or politicians. It was fought – is being fought, and will be fought – in a woman's heart.

It's the patient, long-suffering battle for her children's wellbeing, and it is fought from cradle to grave.

The greatest battle that ever was fought. For our children!

Friday – December 6

IMAGINE coming up with something everyone in the world wanted. Now, imagine you couldn't charge for it. What would you do?

William E. Holler was a sales manager for Chevrolet cars. He was training sales people when he said, "One thing everybody in the world wants is friendliness."

Perhaps you know people who wouldn't appreciate friendliness. I'd suggest we might need to offer different types.

If friendliness isn't in universal demand, then it must be closer to it than anything other than love.

Could you offer that? And, lacking any prospect of payment other than appreciation and friendship in return, would you?

Saturday – December 7

GRANNY MAGGIE used to offer me advice when I was younger. I wonder if you've heard it.

If I was after more pudding, she might give me a slice of bread, saying, "Cherry cake and crusts together will do your stomach good."

What she meant was that the digestive system needs roughage as well as sweetness. Too much of one was just as unhealthy as too much of the other.

The same is true of the days of our lives. Taking the rough with the smooth provides balance, flexibility and appreciation.

I think of dear old Granny Maggie and her home-grown wisdom every time I eat cherry cake – or a crust!

Remember the meaning of the festive season – love.

Winter in the Carpathians, Ukraine.

Sunday – December 8

WHEN I think of Christmas,
I see soft white glistening snow;
I hear carols from King's College
Come on the radio.

I see decorated Christmas trees,
And log fires all aglow,
As, again, we tell that story
Which began so long ago.

Where a baby in a manger
Was born so God could show
How much he cares for all of us
More than we'll ever know.

John Darley

Monday – December 9

THE work of Rumi, the Persian poet and Sufi mystic, is vastly more popular in the internet age than it ever was in the 13th century when he was alive. His words of wisdom sometimes seem to be everywhere.

An educated and religious man, his spiritual insight and creative output surged when he met Shams Tabrizi. Legend has it that Rumi was sitting reading when Shams asked, "What is this?"

"Something that cannot be understood by the unlearned," Rumi replied.

Shams threw his books into a pond. Rumi fished them out again and was amazed to find them dry.

"What is this?" he asked.

"Something that cannot be understood by the learned," Shams replied.

The two men taught and learned together for years after that, before Shams disappeared.

What do I take from all of that? Firstly, that God will do his best work through friends. And secondly, we can read all we like about faith and religion, but we will learn so much more about them if we live them with an open heart and an inquiring mind.

Tuesday – December 10

BROTHER LAWRENCE was a "lay brother" in a monastery in the 17th century. His example and reputation were such that people wrote to him from all across France seeking advice on living a holier life.

He commented to a friend after one such request.

"She seems to me full of goodwill, but she wants to go faster than grace. One does not become holy all at once."

Whatever we hope to do – hopefully something to improve us – we could do a lot worse than proceed at the speed of grace.

Wednesday – December 11

SHE can be difficult at times. At other times she can be a complete delight.

It was the Lady Of The House who made the connection.

"She's always so much better when her sister has been to visit."

I wondered why.

"Well," my sweetheart mused. "I suppose she knows her sister loves her. With the rest of us, she's not so sure, so her defences go up."

What would it be like if we were sure of each other, sure that even if we don't love them, then at least that we genuinely wish them all the best?

How would they know that? We would have to demonstrate it.

Thursday – December 12

MISSING his cousin Minnie Balfour, Robert Louis Stevenson wrote a poem in which he envies her hand-glass the sight of her face.

He describes her mirror as "a thing that has no worth until you lend it something of your grace". In that way, her mirror, he suggests, is better off for her using it.

We have an effect on everything we use, every person we meet, and every gathering we join (or don't join).

We might reflect on that a while, and try to ensure our impact is always one of grace.

Friday – December 13

HARRY lost his footing on the frost recently. A big man, he went down with a thump. Thankfully, he was more embarrassed than hurt.

Still, I checked on him the next morning.

"I was sitting on the side of the bed this morning," he told me. "And I realised I had grazed my knee. Looking at it, I tried to remember the last time it had looked like that.

"Suddenly I felt like I was a ten-year-old again. It was worth the going down to come up again feeling like that!"

Saturday – December 14

TO the amazement of many, she has run the high-street toy shop for several years now.

Her young customers, loyal devotees, know nothing about competition from the internet or paying rates.

They simply love being there, and she loves spoiling them in the little play area the shop provides.

Given that she makes so little money, people wonder why she bothers.

A few know she suffered the greatest loss a parent can experience when her adult son "stepped away", and they don't grudge her the chance to make other children happy.

Never judge another's "foolishness" without also searching their heart for its hurts.

Sunday – December 15

JOHN BANNISTER TABB was an American who taught English and trained for the priesthood around the end of the 1800s.

He penned a short verse called "A Child's Prayer". And I can't help but think adults might benefit from it, too. It reads:

"Make me, dear Lord, polite and kind
To everyone, I pray.
And may I ask you how you find
Yourself, dear Lord, today?"

Monday – December 16

RYAN picked his grandson up and said, "Aidan, do you know something? I –"

The little boy, not yet three years old but quick on the uptake, interrupted by saying, "Love!"

Then he booped his grandad's nose with his finger and added, "You!"

"It's no surprise he could finish that sentence," Ryan told me. "He hears it often enough. I never heard it from my parents, so I did something different for the following generations."

The way a thing always was isn't the way it always has to be.

Tuesday – December 17

OLD wisdom suggests that if you only have two pennies, you should buy a loaf with one and a flower with the other.

The point being that we need to live, but we should also have something to raise living above mere existence.

I thought of that when I saw an uncredited list of "Gifts I Wish I Could Give".

They included, "All the time you need to do all the things you want", "The apology you deserve but never got", "Freedom from fear", "Permission to be imperfect" and "A funny pair of socks".

Wednesday – December 18

THE book, published in the USA in the 1940s, is called "A Treasury Of The Familiar". The publishers gathered excerpts from what they thought were the best artistic, political and humanitarian thoughts in that country's history. It's a wonderful read.

It occurred to me, though, that we, too, often take the familiar for granted. How much good advice have I been offered?

How many words of wisdom have been passed down to me? Because they came from family members, I never thought of them as treasure, and it's too late now to build a chest to keep them in.

Don't disparage the wisdom and kindness of friends and family. Find your own way to keep them close to your heart.

Sending love and support down the generations is something anyone can do.

SILENT movie star Harold Lloyd had what was regarded as the most decorated tree in the world.

It was actually three trees joined together, but very little tree was actually visible.

It stood 20 feet high, was 30 feet around, and had over 800 decorations from all around the world.

The Peanuts character Charlie Brown famously took the last tree in the lot – a small, broken, scraggly thing – and used it to search for the meaning of Christmas.

I hope you have a nice tree, decorated with personal touches. But don't worry about it if you don't, and likewise, don't feel you need to overdo it with the tree or any of the other trappings.

Your Christmas won't be measured by the height of your tree or the glitter of your decorations. It will be measured by the love in your heart and how you share it.

All the rest is . . . well, decoration!

Friday – December 20

I'M not having a proper Christmas this year," she told me. "The last couple of Christmases all but reduced me to tears."

I was struck by her use of the word "proper". Great-aunt Louisa's diaries described a proper Christmas of her childhood.

Sunday best was worn to the station and relatives joined them on the steam train. From a station in the middle of nowhere, they travelled by cart to her grandparents' house.

Christmas Eve was spent preparing.

Christmas Day was spent praying, reading the Bible, and singing hymns. Boxing Day might have games.

Presents were not really a part of what was, primarily, a time of worship.

Wonderful, but quite different from today's celebrations.

I advised my friend there was no such thing as a proper Christmas.

Instead, she should create a new idea of "proper", and make it one that included friends, was centred around love, and that filled her heart with hope.

A CANDLE was lit, wax dripped on to a saucer, and the candle fixed to it.

It was assumed that children could walk upstairs to bed with such home-made candle-holders and not set fire to anything.

You don't realise how wobbly a motion walking up stairs is until you watch your shadow animated by candlelight.

There's the feeling of relief that comes from placing the saucer on the bedside table.

Then the child would carefully measure the distance. He or she needed to be close enough to the candle to be able to blow the flame out, but close enough to the security of the blankets to be fully wrapped up before the light completely departed.

Then a quick prayer and to sleep.

In the morning, if your house had electricity, perhaps the supply would have been restored. In generations before that would not have been an option.

Children, if they could, stayed wrapped up, listening to the sounds of Mum or Dad kindling the fire.

When the noise moved to the kitchen, they knew a warm glow was to be found in the hearth and they could venture downstairs again.

These memories came as I thought about the winter solstice and how it was celebrated by almost every ancient culture around the world.

In the shortest days, be a light-bringer.

Sunday – December 22

HE asked his Sunday school teacher if he could be in the Nativity play.

She said all the roles were filled, so he asked if he could play a character from his favourite computer game "Fortnite".

She said there were no "Fortnite" characters in the Nativity.

He replied that there were no Christmas trees or electric lights, either.

If you wondered why that Nativity play had four wise men . . .

Monday – December 23

SEVERAL years ago we bought a Christmas tree in a pot. The theory was that, still being alive, it wouldn't lose needles. Then we could plant it somewhere else, or have it chipped.

After Christmas it was left behind the garden hut – and forgotten about. It survived two years of complete neglect.

Feeling ashamed, I planted it in our front garden. When Christmas came around again, I decorated it.

While I was hanging the decorations, the child of a neighbour came along and I shared the story of the tree.

"I think it deserves decorating after all that," I said.

He gave it some serious consideration.

"I think every tree deserves decorating," he replied.

I thought about all that trees do for us – all that God's creation does for us – and I couldn't disagree.

Tuesday – December 24

THIS year's church Christmas card has a picture from last year's Nativity. It shows a five-year-old boy lying on the straw in front of the manger, pointing skywards, as if at a star.

In front of the stage lies a board painted with the message *Wise men still seek him.*

I found a chance to have a quiet word with the minister.

"I remember this," I told him. "He wasn't supposed to be there. Is this really the best example?"

The minister smiled.

"You're right; he was a nuisance. He shouldn't have been there, but I saw the chance and took it. He was pointing at the overhead projector.

"He's a reminder for me, that if we did find Jesus in all his glory, there would be nothing left to do," he explained. "So I suggest we are all in the same position as this little fellow. All imperfect. All in the straw at the foot of the manger. All still needing to look for something, even if we don't know it's him."

"In other words," I said as understanding dawned, "the perfect example."

Wednesday – December 25

BEFORE she opens a present or visits anyone this morning, Jane tells me she will spend some time with her jewellery box.

"There's nothing in there of any great financial value," she admits, "but almost everything in it was given to me by good friends or people who loved me: my parents, my children, my dear departed husband.

"Each piece tells a story of the person who gave it. And before I open another gift, I say a prayer of thanks for the gifts of such wonderful people in my life."

Thursday – December 26

BOXING DAY has a long tradition as a celebration in its own right.

Some think it began in grand houses, where servants would be expected to work every Christmas Day, so that the lords and ladies of the land could feed and entertain their friends.

Then, on the following day, the servants would have their day off, and all the leftover food would be boxed up and sent home with them.

What a treat that would have been for their families!

For Mandy, this year, her "boxing day" came a week before Christmas, when she wrapped and labelled several bags of boxes and delivered them to a local charity.

For Sheena, it was when the parents of the children at the school where she was a teacher brought in extra gifts to be distributed among the children whose families were struggling at Christmastime.

For the lucky ones amongst us, Boxing Day, or at least part of it, might be spent folding up the multitude of cardboard boxes our children's gifts came in, then stuffing them into an already full recycling bin.

If boxes have played a notable part in your festive celebrations this year, then, this Boxing Day, perhaps you might take a moment to be thankful.

What can we do to help those who had no boxes beneath their tree?

A BENCH on a hill in the grounds of Cornell University, in the state of New York, reads, *To those who shall sit here rejoicing, to those who shall sit here mourning, sympathy and greeting; so have we done in our time.*

It was donated by graduates who remembered their time there as students.

It also reminds the rest of us that there will be bad times and good. And when we are in the midst of something, we will also one day look back on it.

Saturday – December 28

YOU might have seen one of the many pictures – cleared roads, sometimes in Scandinavia, sometimes in Canada – where the snow on either side is several times the height of the traffic.

But it was a comment by a friend that caught my attention.

"One flake at a time," he said. "It all adds up."

Those snowflakes, by themselves, seem insignificant, but given enough of them . . .

Our habitual actions are like those snowflakes: nothing much in themselves, but building up over the years.

We need to ask, are our "snowflakes" pretty and positive, or a little on the slushy side?

Sunday – December 29

DO you ever spontaneously burst into song? Or feel like it for no reason you can understand?

The mediaeval Christian mystic Mechthild of Magdeburg, in her poem "Effortlessly", suggested one possible cause.

Love, flowing from God to us, might cause that feeling.

She imagined the Holy Spirit as a harpist and us as the harp-strings.

"And all the strings which are touched in love," she wrote, "must sound."

Go on. Feel the touch. And give voice to that feeling.

L AST night we had a power cut,
Sudden, without warning;
It lasted through the darkest hours
Until the early morning.
One moment I am sitting there
With lights on and TV,
The next a blackened silence
Makes it hard to hear or see.
It brings an elemental fear –
Though I'm trying to be brave –
Knowing how it must have felt
When man dwelt in a cave.
We take so much for granted:
Plug in, switch on and go,
But when the power's extinguished
We've nothing left to show.
But as I light a candle
And the match gives off its spark,
I feel that God is with me
And won't leave me in the dark.

John Darley

N EIL MUNRO'S novel "The Daft Days", published in 1907, begins on New Year's Day. In a fictional Scottish town, perhaps based on Inveraray, the drunken bell-ringer rang the bells at the wrong time.

A band paraded through the snowy streets and "women ran out of their houses and crossed the street, some of them, I declare, to kiss each other, for 'tis a fashion lately come, and most genteel, grown wonderfully common in Scotland".

Running out on the morning of New Year's Day to kiss each other might have been "most genteel", and a new tradition, in that setting. But now?

It's a timely reminder that while some traditions last for ever, many come and go. What new tradition – hopefully a loving one – would you like to begin tomorrow?

Happy New Year!

Habits can add up, just like snowflakes – make sure that yours build something positive!